Just Us Girls

48 Creative Art & Craft Projects for Mothers & Daughters to Do Together

CINDY ANN GANADEN

Quarry Books
100 Cummings Center, Suite 406L
Beverly, MA 01915

quarrybooks.com • craftside.typepad.com

First published in the United States of America by
Quarry Books, a member of
Quayside Publishing Group
100 Cummings Center
Suite 406-L
Beverly, Massachusetts 01915-6101
Telephone: (978) 282-9590
Fax: (978) 283-2742
www.quarrybooks.com
Visit www.Craftside.Typepad.com for a behind-the-scenes peek at our crafty world!

Library of Congress Cataloging-in-Publication Data
Ganaden, Cindy Ann.
  Just us girls : 48 creative art projects for mothers and daughters to do together / Cindy Ann Ganaden.
    pages cm
  Includes index.
  ISBN 978-1-59253-890-4 -- ISBN 978-1-61058-936-9 (eISBN)
  1. Handicraft for girls. 2. Mothers and daughters. I. Title.
  TT171.G36 2013
  745.5--dc23

                                                                2013038969

ISBN: 978-1-59253-890-4

Digital edition published in 2014
eISBN: 978-1-61058-936-9

10 9 8 7 6 5 4 3 2 1

Design: Laura McFadden Design, Inc.
Photography: Stefanie Reneé, www.stefanierenee.net

Printed in China

Contents

6 | Introduction

8 | Before We Get Started: Get Into the Foraging Spirit

8 | Some Basic Supplies

10 | An Element for Every Season

14 | **Chapter 1: Spring Introduction :: Earth**

16 | Garden Wish Flags

18 | Floral Nature Crowns

20 | Grass Garden Skirt

22 | Butterfly & Fairy Catcher

24 | Spoon Garden Markers

26 | Natural Potions: Rose Water

28 | Sunburst

30 | Travel Watercolor Kit

32 | Flower Seed Kindness Bombs

34 | **Chapter 2: Summer Introduction :: Fire**

36 | Beachy Natural Jewelry and Hair Accessories

38 | Dream Catchers

40 | Miniature Shadow Box

42 | Natural Tie-Dye

44 | Fairytown: Mud Brick, Bark Teepee, Stick Cabin

48 | Summer Fairies & Garden Gnomes

52 | Nature Wands

54 | Wand Belt

56 | The Huntress: Bow & Arrows

59 | The Huntress: Arm Guard & Quiver

62 | **Chapter 3: Autumn Introduction :: Air**

64 | Leaf & Pod Stamping Prints

66 | Nature Scavenger Hunt: Hunting Cards

68 | Nature Scavenger Hunt: Treasure Box

70 | Walking Sticks

72 | Totem Poles

74 | Fairy Wind Chimes

76 | Punched Tin-Can Lanterns

78 | Wind Sock Chandelier

80 | Rock Games

82 | Lightbulb Hot-Air Balloon Ornament

84 | **Chapter 4: Winter Introduction :: Water**

86 | Badge & Ribbon Medallions

88 | Salt Dough Crafts

90 | Woodland Animal Masks

92 | Happy Thoughts Jar

94 | Don't You Worry Doll

96 | Pocket Sticker Book

98 | Tiny Lavender Flower Doll & Bed

102 | String Art Board

104 | Spool Gift-Tag Ornament

106 | Peaceful Mind Globe

108 | Resources

110 | Acknowledgments

112 | About the Author

113 | Tear-outs

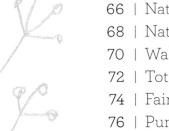
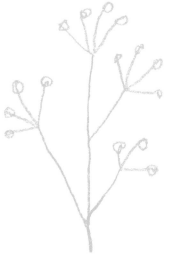

INTRODUCTION

Growing up I loved to draw, craft, and create works of art using treasures I found during my outdoor excursions in the woods near my house. I would return home with pockets full of pebbles, leaves, flowers, and bits of tree bark and twigs. These were my beautiful, natural treasures!

To this day (and now as a mom) whenever we go on vacation, my daughter and I fill our suitcases with natural keepsakes to remind us of our time there. We leave with a promise to use our found treasures in future craft projects that we will make together.

This book is filled with fun activities that my daughter and I have come to enjoy using our shells, sea glass, and driftwood that we gathered and amassed during our many fun filled day trips and summer vacations of years past. We used pinecones, moss, twigs, rocks, and sticks that we foraged and saved during an amazing week spent at Lair of the Bear (Family Camp) in the Stanislaus National Forest. Included are acorns, pods, leaves, bark, and branches collected on our many walks down to the village on the Mountclair Railroad Trail. And we used flowers, leaves, and sticks gathered and collected right here in our backyard, neighborhood, and local trails and parks. Not only did we use a ton of natural materials, but we also used simple home items that we had tucked away in drawers, cupboards, and closets. We also incorporated common materials, like tin cans, glass jars, mint tins, and shoe boxes, which are often overlooked and discarded.

Now as a mom, I'm glad to pass down and share my joy of making, crafting, and creating from all of the materials we've foraged and gathered along the way. There's something incredibly rewarding and satisfying about making art and objects from the materials you've found, collected, and carried home with you. And I am thrilled beyond words that I get to share these experiences with my daughter.

I hope you'll enjoy making crafting memories with your daughter too!

XO

Cindy Ann

P.S. Let's keep in touch! Send me pictures of your projects at CindyAnn@BluPenny.com and you just might see them make a guest appearance on my blog, BluPenny.com.

Before We Get Started: Get Into the Foraging Spirit

We are surrounded by beautiful craft materials. Just look around, and get inspired! We often overlook the little things that can be transformed into creative, functional, memorable art projects. Consider items you run across in your everyday life: that discarded object you passed on the way to school, the wrapper you crumpled up in your pocket, the torn piece of fabric you were going to toss in the trash, or a button that fell off of an old shirt. You'll be surprised what you find when you take a closer look at the world around you and consider the potential in these common, found objects. These hidden treasures can be transformed into unique crafts, and the process of foraging for materials is all part of the fun.

Some Basic Supplies

Embroidery Floss This colorful thread comes in every color of the rainbow! You can find embroidery floss at most craft stores. Wrap your floss around a clothespin to keep it nice, tidy, and tangle-free.

Hot Glue This is an awesome adhesive that dries fast and can be applied to so many different materials. But be careful! When using a hot glue gun, you can easily burn yourself if you are not careful, and it only takes a moment to dry and harden.

Accessories and Embellishments Add a little sparkle to your natural treasures with gems, beads, buttons, glitter, feathers, jewels, sequins, and more. What girl doesn't like a little dazzle?

Acrylic Craft Paint This affordable, versatile paint comes in a full range of colors, including pastels, fluorescents, and iridescents. The small bottles are convenient to store and are easy to squeeze.

Let's hunt and gather!

Here is a list of natural and recycled materials to collect so you can begin creating the crafts in this book:

- tree bark
- leaves
- twigs
- seed pods
- sticks and twigs
- pinecones
- pine needles

- stones
- pebbles
- shells
- sea glass
- seeds
- driftwood

- walnut shells
- acorns
- acorn caps
- feathers
- sand
- moss
- bottle caps

- thimbles
- toothpicks
- popsicle sticks
- scrap fabric
- tin cans
- keys

- baby food, condiment, and sauce jars
- cardboard shoe boxes
- old lightbulbs
- wire hangers
- egg cartons

- mint tins
- clothespins
- wooden spools
- chenille stems (*also known as pipe cleaners*)

Scissors A good set of scissors make cutting through fabric and paper a breeze. Don't skimp out! Go out and get yourself a good pair.

Markers, Pens, Pencils, and Pastels Look in drawers, purses, and book bags. You can probably find all you need and avoid going to the store.

All the Extras Are Right Here Jump-start your creativity! In the back of this book, you will find tear-out materials pages to incorporate in many of these projects.

Decoupage Wheat Paste Wheat paste has been used for hundreds of years as an adhesive. It's easy to make, inexpensive, and nontoxic. You can purchase decoupage at your local craft store, or with a few simple supplies, you can make your own (see right). Wheat paste easily sticks to just about any porous surface and dries to a rock-hard finish.

You'll Need:

- 1 cup (125 g) flour
- 4 cups (950 ml) water
- 2 packets unflavored gelatin
- 1 tablespoon (13 g) sugar
- 3 drops peppermint oil extract
- whisk or spoon to stir with
- saucepan
- mason jar or airtight container

Make Your Own Decoupage Wheat Paste

Make your own decoupage wheat paste as an alternative to commercial decoupages. This nontoxic formula is simple to prepare and friendly for the home. We love how it adheres with ease and produces a durable finish. You probably already have the ingredients in your kitchen, so why not get started? The recipe is a 1:4 ratio.

Make It!

1. In a saucepan over medium-low heat, combine the water and gelatin until dissolved.
2. Slowly add in the flour. Stir continuously for 5 to 10 minutes until you get a smooth, creamy consistency. Be sure not to let it boil.
3. Add in the sugar and peppermint oil and stir until combined.

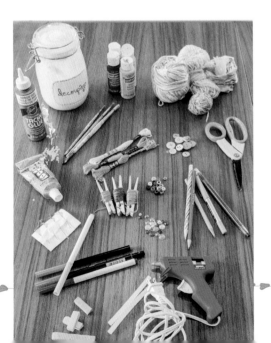

An Element for Every Season

Tap into your natural crafting element. Which element best captures your crafting spirit? Are you an earth, fire, air, or water girl? Use these pages as a reference as you craft through this book.

It's All So Elemental

Air moves us,

Fire transforms us,

Water shapes us,

Earth heals us.

And the balance of the wheel goes 'round and 'round.

And the balance of the wheel goes 'round.

—by Cathleen Shell, Cybele, Moonsea, and Prune

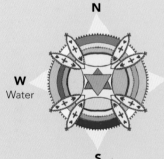

Earth
N

W
Water

E
Air

S
Fire

SPRING EARTH: Symbolic of All Life

An earth girl is kind and warm—she always welcomes her friends and family with a big hug. She loves to laugh and is the type of girl who creates long-lasting friendships. She is faithful and sometimes overprotective and stubborn, refusing to change her mind even when she knows she's wrong. She is deeply rooted by the love of her home. She likes to stay in her comfort-zone. An earth girl learns by doing and believes in things that she can see and touch because she knows they are real. To stay balanced, she should add fire, water, and air elements to her life.

Earth Qualities: *patient, faithful, reliable, strong, grounded, practical, and stubborn*

Season: Spring: *Spring Icons: birds, butterflies, bunnies, baby chicks, watering can, nest, eggs, snails, raindrops, rainbows, shamrocks, daffodils, green grass, budding plants, and flowers*

Direction: *north*

Earth Colors: *yellows, browns, earth tones, greens, and black*

Zodiac Signs: *Taurus, Capricorn, Virgo*

Earth Animals:

bear: bravery, courage, confidence, nurturing

cat: cleverness, independence, watchfulness, mystery

deer: love, grace, swiftness, beauty, creativity

dog: loyalty, cooperation, helpfulness, resourcefulness

elephant: reliability, dignity, royal, pride, happiness

fox: quick thinking, adaptability, cleverness, strategy

mouse: super awareness, determination, innocence, groundedness

tiger: protection, generosity, energy, wealth

wolf: intelligence, cunning, friendliness, compassion

Earth Tree Woods: *ash: justice, fortune* **elm:** *girl power* **maple:** *strength, wisdom* **cypress:** *protection*

Earth Stones: *Earth stones are opaque and bright. They help you stay grounded and gain confidence: jade, turquoise, emerald, quartz, onyx.*

SUMMER FIRE: Symbolic of Energy, Power, Passion, Creativity, Creation, Rebirth, Renewal, and Action

A fire girl is a passionate, natural leader. She has a charming personality that lights up a room. Her personality is so magnetic that she is exciting to be around. She's an independent thinker and always follows her gut. Once she makes up her mind, there's no changing it. She's very athletic and doesn't let anything hold her back. However, sometimes all of the excitement can go to her head, and she can unintentionally hurt others' feelings. As a fire girl, she has the gift of transformation and can turn any negative into a positive by taking on all the other elements.

Fire Qualities: *courageous, daring, fun, mischievous, enthusiastic, passionate, and creative*

Season: Summer: *Summer Icons: sun, seashells, waves, mermaids, campfires, hikes, daisies, strawberries, watermelon, sunflowers, full garden, picnic, flip flops, sailboats, ice pops, and bathing suits*

Direction: *south*

Fire Colors: *reds and pinks*

Zodiac Signs: *Leo, Sagittarius, Aries*

Fire Animals:

dragonfly: *prosperity, luck, strength, peace, harmony*
firefly: *inspiration, patience, attraction, aspiration, guidance*
hedgehog: *cool and calm, intuitition, resourcefulness, intelligence*
horse: *power, grace, nobility, strength, ambition*
lion: *courage, wiseness, royalty, loyalty, protection*
salamander: *keen intellect, faith, purity*
thunderbird: *unbeatable spirit, power, expansive*
ram: *heart, passion, creativity*
rooster: *watchfulness, courage, fighting spirit, reliability*
dragon: *action, adaptability, success, warmth, admiration*

Fire Tree Woods: oak: *juniper: healing, protection* **oak:** *fire, success, strength and courage, money, longevity* **pine:** *immortality, abundance, rebirth* **rosewood:** *love, union, healing*

Fire Stones: Fire stones have a positive influence and help you recharge: *amber, ruby, red garnet, diamond, tiger's eye*

AUTUMN AIR: Symbolic of Life, but Also Represents Unity, Freedom, Eternity, and Balance

An air girl loves to tell stories—she constantly has her head in the clouds living in her own dream world. She's always up for an adventure and doesn't like to be tied down. She's a free thinker with an overactive imagination. She likes to break the rules. She is a brilliant book worm who always comes up with a clever solution, but sometimes she tends to think more then she feels. At times, she can lack social grace. As an air girl, she can balance her free-spirited nature by focusing on practicality and making an extra effort to relate to her family and friends.

Air Qualities: *carefree, trusting, optimistic, kind-hearted, independent, and cunning*

Season: Autumn: *Autumn Icons: falling leaves, red maple leaves, acorns, harvest, pumpkins, corn, mushrooms, wheat, nuts and berries, owls, spiders, darkness, and harvest moon (full moon)*

Direction: *east*

Colors: *whites, creams, and blues*

Zodiac Signs: *Gemini, Libra, Aquarius*

Air Animals:
butterfly: reawakening, transformation, celebration, light
dove: love, grace, promise, devotion, hope
eagle: guardianship, free, vision, skill, determination
falcon: spirit, light, focus, aspiration, determination
hummingbird: joy, playfulness, affection, loyalty, agility
owl: wisdom, mystery, intelligence, protection
peacock: pride, glory, vision, royalty
swan: beauty, dreams, balance, elegance, partnership

Feathers: *truthful, speedy, light, ideal for flight and ascension*

Wings: *able to rise above challenges, divine*

Air Tree Woods: *aspen: intuition and communication* **apple:** *love, beauty, peace, healing happiness. (Did you know that this tree is associated with unicorns?)*
cedar: prosperity, self-control **hickory:** *balance, nourishment, good intentions*

Air Stones: *Air stones are transparent and semitransparent and come in shades of white, gold, pink, and blue. They encourage quick thinking and help you become more flexible, mobile, and social: sapphire, amethyst, topaz, smoky quartz.*

WINTER WATER: Symbolizes Purity, Fertility, Wisdom, Transformation, Motion, Reflection, Intuition, Renewal, and Life

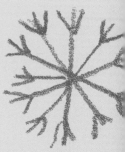

A water girl goes with the flow and follows her heart. She feels everything deeply and embraces everyone with an open heart. She's a hopeless romantic, and because of this, she often finds herself tearful and broken-hearted. She's super artistic and highly sensitive. She tends to go overboard and change her mind as often as the tides. She's the friend who will always listen—an eternal optimist who sees everything through rose-colored glasses. As a water girl, she can balance her overflowing emotions by grounding herself and taking the time to temper her decisions with a dose of rationale.

Water Qualities: *trusting, devoted, compassionate, understanding, open-hearted, modest, and creative*

Season: Winter: *Winter Icons: snow, snowflakes, skiing, sledding, pine trees, chestnuts, yule log, oak tree, mistletoe, ivy, candle, warm fire, pomegranates, apples, pine cones, night sky, stars, and bells*

Direction: *west*

Colors: *blues, greens, and turquoise*

Zodiac Sign: *Cancer, Scorpio, Pisces*

Water Animals:
dolphin: playfulness, friendliness, harmony, community
fish: creativity, happiness, knowledge, femininity
frog: luck, dreams, opportunity, renewal, transformation
octopus: will, focus, complex, mystery, flexibility
seahorse: patience, friendliness, protection, sharing, persistence
turtle: creativity, patience, strength, stability, endurance
whale: well-being, nurturing, sensitivity, perception

Water Tree Woods: *birch:* *purification, health, new beginnings* **eucalyptus:** *healing* *mesquite: nurturing and providing* *willow: intuition*

Water Stones: *Water stones are semitransparent and can change color. They dissolve and carry away negative energy and emotions: opal, moonstone, pear, coral, aquamarine.*

1

SPRING INTRODUCTION

Earth

Birds are popping their heads out of their nests and beginning to sing their spring songs. Flowers are blossoming, and the sun is lingering around longer so we have more time outdoors to play. Spring is a great time of the year for just us girls to witness nature's rebirth by getting outdoors and making some Garden Wish Flags, Grass Garden Skirts, Spoon Garden Markers, and other natural crafts.

You'll Need

- 5 pieces of colored or patterned fabric approximately 10" × 8" (20.5 × 25.5 cm) that will be used as the base background flag
- 5 pieces of white cotton or muslin fabric approximately 6½" × 5½" (16.5 × 14 cm) for vertical layout, 4¼" × 7¾" (11 × 20 cm) for horizontal layout)
- Embroidery floss
- Buttons
- Small bells
- Ribbon and trim
- Yarn or cord for hanging
- Fabric markers, paint, crayons, and stamps
- Scissors and/or pinking shears
- Fabric glue
- Tapestry needle

Garden Wish Flags

Garden wish flags are the perfect way to send dreams and wishes into the breeze. Wish for hope, love, peace, strength, wisdom, or even a raindrop or two to nourish your garden. These garden wish flags are inspired by the traditional Tibetan prayer flags that can be found at the base of the Himalaya Mountains.

Mother & Daughter: *Wish flags are a great birthday activity. Each of your guests can write or draw a message for the birthday girl! String the flags and create party decorations that you can save and hang in your daughter's room.*

Make It!

1. Choose a flag layout, horizontal (Dar-Ding) or vertical (Dar-Cho), and cut the fabric to the appropriate sizes.

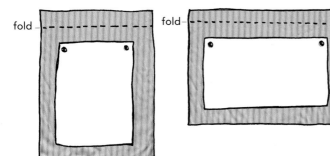

2. Fold 1¼" (3 cm) of the top of your colored/patterned fabric over and glue the edge to the back of the flag, leaving a thin pocket for threading yarn or cord.

3. Draw, write, paint, and stamp your message on the white fabric. Keep it positive! (Check out our suggestions.)

4. Sew the white fabric with your message to your background fabric with embroidery floss.

5. Embellish the flags with ribbons, buttons, and bells.

6. Thread yarn or cord through the back of the flags, leaving enough thread on either side to hang up flags.

Flag Raising: The best time to hang new wish flags is in the mornings on sunny, windy days. Hang them in your backyard or garden where they will sway and catch the breeze.

Color Coordinate: Match your background fabric color to an element! Arrange your wish flags from left to right in order of: sky and air (*whites, creams,* and *blues*), fire (*reds* and *pinks*), water (*greens* and *turquoises*), or earth (*yellows, browns,* and *earth tones*). Position your personal symbol/animal in the middle to provide harmony and to balance the elements. Refer to the "An Element for Every Season" section in the front of the book for more symbolic meaning and information on earth, fire, air, and water.

Did You Know? Tibetan prayer flags come in sets of five and contain writing and images meant to generate peace and good wishes. The flags usually incorporate colors and symbols representing all the elements.

- Hope
- Make Connections
- Love
- More Trees
- World Peace
- Happiness
- Hugs
- There is Enough for Everyone
- Freedom
- Sharing is Caring
- Harvest Life
- Wish Big
- Be Brave
- Give Thanks
- Dream Big
- Be Fearless
- Smile
- Create Beauty
- Laugh Out Loud
- Start Now
- Remember, Learn, Forgive
- Let Go
- Listen to Your Heart
- Give

Tip
Don't worry about frayed edges. These flags are designed to dissolve in the wind.

Floral Nature Crowns

Spring is finally here! Celebrate nature's rebirth with a fresh floral nature crown. You never know who will join you for spring festivities: woodland fairies, butterflies, and baby birds all love to welcome spring, too.

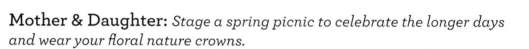

Mother & Daughter: *Stage a spring picnic to celebrate the longer days and wear your floral nature crowns.*

You'll Need

- 30 or more freshly picked flowers, approximately 5" to 7" (13 to 18 cm) long
- 4 to 5 stems of green leaves approximately 5" to 7" (13 to 18 cm) long
- Floral wire, green embroidery floss, or string
- Floral tape (optional)
- Floral shears or scissors
- Ribbon

Make It!

1. Go on a hike or take a walk to collect your flowers and greenery.

2. Remove excess leaves and buds. You want clean stems with blooms at the top.

3. Make a base crown. Measure the circumference of your head and start overlapping three to four stems of green leaves. Layer one on top of the other. Every few inches, secure the stems with floral wire or embroidery floss. You want to end up making one long stalk of greenery.

4. Create eight to ten flower bundles. Pair up small groups of flowers and tie them together with floral wire, tape, or embroidery floss.

5. Embellish the base with the flower bundles by overlapping and tightly securing each bundle to the base using floral wire or embroidery floss. Continue laying bundles in the same direction. Be sure the blooms face outward and the greenery is not "trapped."

6. Shape your crown. Tie a ribbon to each end of the crown and then gently bend and shape your crown into a circle. Secure the ribbons into a bow.

7. Reinforce the crown and binding with thread or floral wire. Cover the closure with blooms. Flowers will also hide any imperfections. Spray your crown with water or keep it in a cool place until you're ready to wear it.

Some flowers to consider using:

- daisies
- wildflowers
- baby's breath
- buttercups
- clover
- morning glories
- dandelions
- lisyanthus
- carnations
- statice
- iris
- freesia
- lavender

Tip

Preserve and Dry Your Crown: After a day of wearing and playing with your crown, hang it on a doorknob to dry. Then use it as a decoration for your room.

You'll Need

- 1 to 2 bags of raffia ribbon
- Jute rope or string
- A variety of 15 or more freshly picked flowers, approximately 2" to 3" (5 to 7.5 cm) long
- 5 to 6 large green leaves or vines
- Scissors
- Floral wire, green embroidery floss, or string
- Tapestry needle

Grass Garden Skirt

Evoke the spirit of the Pacific islands with a sweet grass garden skirt. And remember to dance! Twirl your grass garden skirt to a beat—tell a story through your movements so your skirt can rustle in the breeze as you dance the afternoon away.

Mother & Daughter: *Aloha! Host a luau and encourage everyone to help you create a dance story.*

Make It!

1. Wrap the rope around your waist 1½ times, and then cut it.

2. Measure and cut your raffia into strips approximately 36" (91.5 cm) long.

3. Loop and secure the raffia around the rope. Fold each strand in half and pinch the top to make a small loop. Place that loop under the rope and then pull the strand ends through the loop. Pull it tight to make a knot, securing each raffia strand around the rope.

4. Embellish with flowers and greenery. Use floral wire or a needle and embroidery floss to evenly space and attach your flower blooms and leaves to the jute rope waistband.

Tips

Add more color to your skirt by using alternating colors of raffia.

Mist frazzled and wrinkled raffia with water and gently reshape it with your hands.

You'll Need

- A sturdy stick approximately 14" (36 cm) long
- Mineral oil or furniture wax
- 24" (61 cm) of 12-gauge wire (a wire hanger also works)
- Wire cutter
- A piece of mesh, cheesecloth, or muslin fabric
- Scissors
- Tapestry needle and embroidery floss
- Duct tape
- Sandpaper
- Carving knife
- Scrap fabric, ribbon, or string
- Masking tape
- Paint

Butterfly & Fairy Catcher

Catch hours of outdoor enjoyment and experience the thrill of examining nature's little wonders. Spend some time with these delicate creatures—then return them to their homes so others can enjoy their beauty.

Mother & Daughter: *Write about the butterflies and fairies you caught in a journal. What are their names? Do they have a favorite flower? What colors and shapes are their wings?*

Make It!

CHOOSE AND PREPARE YOUR STICK

1. Select a fairly straight, sturdy stick that won't bend or break easily. Remember, some trees have magical properties, so refer to the "An Element for Every Season" section on page 10 to see which ones suit you best.

2. Clean it, strip off any excess bark, and then sand the branch smooth. Use a carving knife to strip away knots and other imperfections.

3. Seal the stick with mineral oil or furniture wax.

MAKE THE NET

1. Cut your fabric into an obtuse isosceles triangle (See A).

2. Fold over 1" (2.5 cm) on the long side and sew a pocket for the wire to go through.

3. Fold your triangle in half and sew the edges together with needle and floss to form the net.

4. Thread the wire through the net pocket, bending it into a circle as you go.

5. Twist the wire ends together to close the circle.

6. Use the remaining extended wire to attach the net to the stick, using masking tape to secure it in place.

7. Conceal the masking tape with scraps of fabric or ribbon (See B).

8. Decorate the stick with loose fabric for streamers. Now you're ready to catch some fairies and butterflies (See C).

B

C

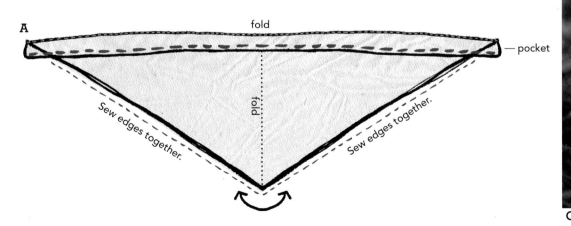

A

fold

— pocket

Sew edges together.

fold

Sew edges together.

Spoon Garden Markers

Personalize your garden and add some vintage flair with whimsical markers created from old spoons! These spoon garden markers will help you remember where you planted each herb, spice, or flower so you can water and fertilize your garden with confidence.

You'll Need

- Old spoons
- Tear-out plant marker labels (pages 115 & 117)
- Hammer
- Pencil and paper
- Waterproof fine-tip black marker
- Markers and colored pencils in various colors
- Paint
- Decoupage
- Cotton balls
- Rubbing alcohol
- Scissors or craft knife

Mother & Daughter: *Give your garden oasis a name by using a spoon marker to stake your claim on your garden. Don't forget to include symbols and imagery when naming your garden.*

Make It!
PREPARE THE SPOON

1. Lay the spoon on a firm, hard surface.
2. Holding the handle of the spoon, hammer the spoon until it is flattened. (See Tips on opposite page.)

LABEL YOUR GARDEN MARKERS

1. Before labeling, dampen a cotton ball with rubbing alcohol and clean your flattened spoon.
2. Cut out the supplied plant marker labels on pages 115 and 117 or create your own.
3. Color your labels and write in the plant names with a waterproof fine-tip marker.
4. Decoupage your label onto the head of your spoon.
5. Now you're ready to push the spoon handle into the dirt to label your plants.

Tips

Real sterling silverware is easier to hammer than modern stainless steel flatware.

Hammer both sides to create a nice, flat working surface.

If you plan to draw your own labels, trace around the flattened spoon head to get an idea of the correct size for your image.

Apply several coats of decoupage, waiting until each coat is completely dried, to ensure a waterproof seal.

Explore More:

- Personalize a set of markers and tie them up with a ribbon to make a garden gift.

- Have a garden party! Get into the planting spirit by inviting others over to help you decorate and label your garden.

Natural Potions: Rose Water

Smell sweet as a rose by wearing a luxuriously simple and healthy concoction you can make yourself. Rose water has many benefits besides being used as perfume. You can use it as a natural cleanser or a salve to relieve itchiness from bug bites. Transform your bath into a luxurious home spa with a bit of rose water or sprinkle it on your love notes. You can even add a drop or two to your rice, cakes, or pies.

Mother & Daughter: *Plant a rose bush together so you can harvest your own petals to use in your nature potions. Explore the various types of roses and learn about their care. These delicate beauties require careful nurturing.*

You'll Need

- **Clean rose petals** (If you don't grow your own roses, look for organic roses to make sure they haven't been sprayed with pesticides.)
- Water
- Ice
- Stock pot and lid
- Brick or heavy glass ramekin
- Pie tin or shallow, stainless-steel bowl
- Jars for storing your potions
- Label and lid tear-outs (page 113)

Make It!

1. Place the brick in the center of a deep stock pot. Position the rose petals around the brick, and pour in the water until it reaches to just below the top of the brick.

2. Place the pie tin on top of the brick.

3. Place the lid on the pot upside down and fill it with ice (see A).

4. Bring the contents of the stock pot to a boil, replacing the ice on the lid as it melts. As the rose petals boil, the heat rises and hits the cold lid and causes it to condense and drip down into the pie tin.

5. Once the water and rose petals are at a boil, bring the heat down and simmer for 3 to 4 hours, replacing the ice as needed.

6. Bottle your potions and add decorative labels and lids. See the tear-outs on page 113.

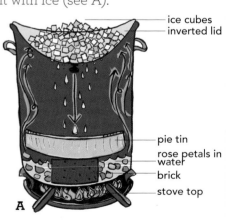

ice cubes
inverted lid
pie tin
rose petals in water
brick
stove top

A

Mixology: Good Potions Always Start with Good Intentions

Brighten someone's day by giving them a bottle of your good intentions. Now that you know how to make rose water, you can create all kinds of natural potions with a pinch of this and a pinch of that. Try chopping up herbs like rosemary, basil, and mint. Zest some oranges, lemons, and grapefruit to make a citrus-scented potion. Or add some lavender to make your own lavender water. Write down your natural potions recipes as you brew and assemble a book to share with your friends.

Sunburst

Sunbursts are an ancient tradition. The four main points represent the four directions (north, south, east and west) and the four elements (earth, fire, air, and water). A sunburst is a good luck charm that is said to give you sweet dreams.

Mother & Daughter: *Create a wisdom circle. Bring together multiple generations of mothers and daughters to work together and take turns weaving. Mom holds and daughter weaves, then switch roles. Working together will make the weaving easier.*

You'll Need:

- 4 sticks approximately 15" to 18" (38 to 46 cm) long and similar in size
- String, yarn, or embroidery floss in 4 to 5 coordinating colors
- Ribbon, lace, or trim for the outer border
- Decorative beads and accessories, such as feathers
- Sandpaper

Make It!

1. Select your sticks. Choose fairly straight, strong (yet pliable) sticks free of notches that are about 15" to 18" (38 to 46 cm) long and not too thick. Remember, certain trees have magical properties. (See the "An Element for Every Season" section on page 10.)

2. Sand off any jagged edges and cross two sticks to make an X.

3. Use string to tie a knot around the intersection of the X.

4. Tightly wrap your string in a figure eight around the intersection, completely covering it.

5. Start weaving your first color. Wrap the string under and over each stick until you finish the center diamond of the sunburst. The amount of rotations required depends on the stick size.

6. Cut the string, leaving a tail that is long enough to tuck under and hold in place.

Tips

Count your rotations if you want each band and color to be the same.

Keep the tension taut so the string doesn't sag but not so tight that you move your X off kilter.

If you make a mistake, just unwind and start over again.

Adjust your sticks as you weave if necessary—be sure to keep them an even distance apart.

Explore More:

For more depth, try alternating recessed and raised rows. Do this by flipping your weaving over and working from the backside. Or, try weaving by twos, skipping every other stick.

7. Repeat steps 2–6 with your second set of sticks, making this diamond slightly larger than the first.

8. Attach the two diamonds together to make your sunburst. Take your time and remember that four hands are sometimes better than two.

   - Lay the two diamonds on top of each other so you have an evenly spaced eight-point sunburst.
   - Tie a string (use a new color) on one of the bottom sticks toward the center.
   - Weave the string over and under, over and under.
   - Make three to four more laps around the diamonds, and then switch to the next color.

9. Continue weaving the design. String beads into some of the outer rays.

10. Make a band of space by wrapping the string around each stick up approximately ½" (1.3 cm) or so and then continue weaving.

11. Finish the sunburst with a border by weaving lace or ribbon.

12. Add final embellishments to the diamond centers and ends, such as feathers, tassels, gems, or pom-poms.

Color Combos

Before you start, consider all of the possible color combinations. Which color will be dominant? How will you arrange the colors? Consider weaving your colors in the elemental order:

Earth (north): yellows and browns

Fire (south): reds and pinks

Air (east): whites, creams, and blues

Water (west): greens and turquoises

You'll Need

- **Small metal tin** (Mint tins are the perfect size.)
- **Oven bake clay** (Try Sculpey and Fimo, available at local craft stores.)
- **4 teaspoons (18.4 g) baking soda**
- **2 teaspoons (5 ml) white vinegar**
- **½ teaspoon light corn syrup**
- **2½ teaspoons (6.7 g) cornstarch**
- **Toothpick for mixing paint**
- **Measuring cup**
- **Food coloring**
- **Rolling pin**
- **Water brush** (Koi Water Brush and Fantastix are great choices.)
- **Pencil or chopstick to create circular wells** (optional)

Travel Watercolor Kit

Create a travel watercolor kit like a plein air artist. Mix your own colors in this small paint box and carry it in your pocket everywhere you go so you can capture the moment. Did you know that artists have been mixing and making their own paints for decades? Now it's your turn.

Tip

Create circular wells by using an eraser end of a pencil or a chopstick to press into the clay.

Mother & Daughter: *Create a custom paint set to take on your next nature adventure. Use your favorite colors to capture the countryside, mountains, oceans, or your own backyard. (These also make great gifts!)*

Make It!

TIN PALETTE

1. Knead the clay until it is warm and pliable and then roll it until it is ½" to ²/₃" (1.3 to 1.7 cm) thick.

2. Press the clay into the clean tin, covering the entire inside. Be sure to push the clay into the tin's corners.

3. Make the paint wells by pressing your thumb firmly into the clay. Evenly space paint wells and be sure not to expose the tin bottom (See A).

4. Bake according to the clay's directions.

5. While your tin palette is cooling, begin mixing watercolors.

Make it!

THE WATERCOLORS

1. Mix the baking soda and vinegar in a measuring cup until it fizzes.

2. Add corn syrup and cornstarch. Mix well until dissolved.

3. Pour the mixture into the paint wells.

4. Add food coloring to each well and mix with a toothpick.

5. Let the paint "set up." This can take 24 to 48 hours. Then you're ready to go.

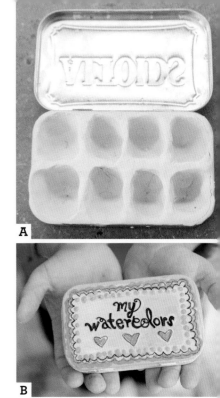

A

B

Explore More:

Decorate and personalize the outside of your travel watercolor kit (see B).

Food Color Mixing Guide

turquoise = 4 drops blue + 1 drop yellow
aqua = 4 drops blue + 1 drop green
chartreuse = 5 drops yellow + 1 drop green
fuchsia = 9 drops red + 1 drop blue
purple = 4 drops blue + 1 drop red
lime green = 6 drops yellow + 1 drop green
orange = 8 drops yellow + 1 drop red

You'll Need

- 5 cups dry, sifted soil
- 4 to 5 packets of seeds native to your area
- 1½ pounds (680 g) air-dry clay
- 1 cup (225 g) of fertilizer like natural humus
- Large bowl or container for mixing
- Cookie sheets

Yield

This recipe makes 12 to 24 Kindness Bombs. If you'd like to make a bigger batch, this recipe is a 5:3:1 ratio: 5 parts soil, 3 parts clay, 1 part seeds, and 1 part fertilizer.

Flower Seed Kindness Bombs

Spread the love and deliver some kindness to your neighborhood by rolling up some of these Flower Seed Kindness Bombs. They are nice for Mother Earth and help beautify your community, too.

Mother & Daughter: *Work together by decorating the Earth one garden at a time—or race to see who can spread the kindness faster.*

Make It!

1. Mix soil and seeds in a container or bowl (See A).

2. Add clay to the mixture.

3. Continue adding more soil until you work up a cookie-dough consistency (See B).

4. Roll the mixture into gumball-size balls and then set on a cookie sheet for drying.

Explore More:

- Make fun shapes! Use cookie cutters to make hearts, stars, and other cool shapes.

- Decorate an egg carton to hold the Kindness Bombs, and you will have a great present for a green thumb (See C).

- Use herbs, salad greens, and edible flowers to grow a cook's garden.

Tips

Drying can take up to 2 to 3 days. Then, you can store them or begin tossing your Kindness Bombs.

Humus is a natural fertilizer.

Some flower and herb seeds to consider

• Poppies	• Baby's Breath	• Daisies	• Cilantro	• Catnip
• Local Wildflowers	• Blue Flax	• Basil	• Chives	• Oats
	• Cornflower	• Dill	• Parsley	• Wheat

SUMMER INTRODUCTION

Fire

What better way is there for us girls to spend summer days (and nights) than creating crafting magic? Cool off from the summer heat with some mermaids, and capture your adventures within a Miniature Shadow Box. Catch your dreams under the summer stars with Dream Catchers. And don't forget to invite the gnomes and fairies over for tea!

Beachy Natural Jewelry and Hair Accessories

Embrace summer all year long with some natural, beachy jewelry. Shells, driftwood, or sea glass—any of these will dress up an outfit and remind you of that great summer vacation at the beach!

You'll Need

- Seashells, coral, sea glass, small pieces of driftwood, silver dollars, and/or starfish
- Hemp cord, embroidery floss, or string to make a necklace
- Jump rings
- Jewelry blanks and hardware
- An assortment of decorative beads and buttons
- Nail polish in various colors
- Clear nail polish
- Needle-nose pliers
- **Craft epoxy** (such as E-6000, found at local craft stores)

Mother & Daughter: *Find two pieces of shell, sea-glass, or driftwood that fit together like a puzzle. Keep one half for yourself and give the other to mom.*

Make It!

1. Take a walk on the beach and gather natural materials.

2. Decide what kind of jewelry you are going to make and select the blanks and hardware. (Check out our Hardware Clinic, opposite.)

2. Clean the shells and driftwood, using mild soap if necessary.

3. Paint your natural treasures with nail polish, using a top coat of clear polish to seal the pieces and add a pretty shine. Allow to dry.

4. Use epoxy to attach the jewelry backing to pieces and let cure for 24 hours.

5. Embellish with beads, buttons, and other extras.

Tips

Experiment with color by painting your whole item one solid color, just painting the bottom edge, or creating an alternating design.

Remember, sometimes the simplest designs are the prettiest. Know when to stop painting and decorating.

Make a locket by using two matching seashells.

Hardware Clinic

Depending on the type of jewelry you'll make, you'll need to choose appropriate hardware.

Pendant necklace: jump rings, string, or a finished chain to hang your pendant

Locket: hinge, jump rings, string, or a finished chain to hang your locket

Brooch: a jewelry pin back bar

Ring: ring blank

Earrings: jump rings and earring blanks

Hair accessories: bobby pins, hair clips with a glue pad, barrettes, and headbands

Bracelet: bracelet blank or a cord and jump rings

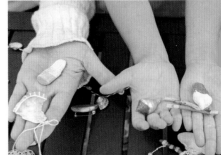

Dream Catchers

Catch your sweet summer dreams with a dream catcher so you can savor them long after the light of morning arrives. Dream catchers have a special way of capturing only the special dreams that you want to remember—the bad ones drift by so you don't give them a second thought.

Mother & Daughter: *Dream catchers are traditionally passed down from mother to daughter. Pass your sweet dreams down to a new baby in your family.*

You'll Need

- Tree limb or vine approximately 26" (66 cm) long
- Strong thread or ribbon
- 3 twist ties
- Decorative accessories (beads, feathers, gemstones, crystals, and trinkets with meaning)
- Scrap fabric, ribbon, yarn, twine, and leather suede cord
- Tapestry needle and embroidery floss or thread
- Center heart tear-out and tags (See the cutouts on pages 137 & 138).
- Hot glue gun and hot glue sticks
- Scissors or craft knife

Make It!

CREATE THE NEVER-ENDING CIRCLE OF LIFE—YOUR HOOP.

1. Select a tree limb. Native Americans traditionally selected a willow branch for its flexibility and ability to connect with the dream world through the water element.

2. Shape your tree limb into a circle. Coil your limb around several times and then use twist ties to secure the limb in three different positions along the hoop.

3. Press your hoop between two heavy books. Allow to dry overnight.

4. Leave your hoop bare or wrap it with scrap fabric, ribbon, or cord. Use a dot of hot glue to secure fabric ends to your hoop.

Tips

Wrap your fabric tightly, overlapping each strand.

Wrap your string around a pencil (like a reel) so it doesn't get tangled as you weave your web.

You may run out of string before you finish your webbing. Just tie off that piece, cover the knot with a bead, and add another string so you can continue weaving the web.

If you are planning on hanging your dream catcher outside, put a coat or two of decoupage or homemade wheat paste on your inner paper hearts to seal them.

WEAVE THE WEB OF LIFE THAT CONNECTS US ALL.

1. Tie a knot at one end of the string, and then tie the string to your hoop. (You'll use this to hang the dream catcher.)

2. Start weaving your first row. Begin at the top of your hoop and work clockwise. Tie hitch knots approximately 2" (5 cm) apart (see A). Evenly space the knots, and keep the string snug as you go from knot to knot, being careful not to distort the string's arching shape.

3. Begin the next row of web. Tie your hitch knots in the middle of the arched string from the previous row (see B). Continue tying hitch knots so the string forms a web with an opening in the center that is about the same size as the heart cutout. Tie it off with a double-knot and cut off the excess.

4. With your tapestry needle and thread, sew your center hearts onto the inner-most web row. You'll need two hearts the same size. One for each side.

5. Tie decorative dangling strands to the bottom of the dream catcher. Hang feathers to represent air and let your dreams freely pass through the web. Write words of encouragement and empowerment to strengthen your dreams and use colored beads and gemstones to represent the four elements and directions.

6. Place the dream catcher near your bedroom window. With the first rays of sunlight, all bad thoughts that entered your mind during the night should disperse.

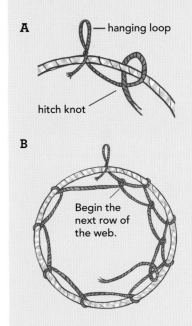

A — hanging loop
hitch knot

B — hanging loop
Begin the next row of the web.

Tie a Hitch Knot

1. Hold string in place and loosely loop it over the top of your hoop.

2. Move string to the back of the hoop to form an arched hole.

3. Pull the string through the hole and start on your next knot.

Colors for Your Dream Catcher

Earth (north): yellows and browns

Fire (south): reds and pinks

Air (east): whites, creams, and blues

Water (west): greens and turquoises

Miniature Shadow Box

Use a mini shadow box to capture a moment, a scene in a dream, or a walk in your favorite fairytale. Create your own mini world: Who would you be? What would you see? Would you swim with the mermaids? (We'll show you how!)

You'll Need

- **A small box** (jewelry box or matchbox)
- **Cut-out character tear-outs** (page 133)
- **Assorted materials** that fit the scene
- **2"(5 cm) medium-gauge wire** (to make characers swim)
- Sand
- Moss
- Burlap twine
- Small seashells
- White glue
- Scissors or craft knife
- Foam brush or Popsicle stick

Mother & Daughter: *Make two! What is your viewpoint? Even the slightest change in perspective can have charming results.*

Make It!

1. Drizzle the glue on the back of the box and spread with a foam brush. (See A)

2. Apply sand. Remove the excess and set aside to dry (See B).

3. If you have any bare spots, add more glue and reapply sand..

4. Choose a background. Use the paper tear-outs provided (see page 133) or your own. Wallpaper and wrapping paper tend to work well.

5. Cut out your characters and lay out the scene. Play with scale and where to place smaller and larger objects. Once you're pleased with the scene, secure it with glue.

6. Decorate the border. We used burlap and twine, but ribbon or chenille stems also work. Remember to add little accents in each corner.

Tip

Make your character swim or fly: Glue wire to the back of your character and background to suspend them.

Tips

Remember, this is your own small world, whether it's a tiny garden, a view from above, or a small nesting hide-away. Draw your own characters to create your own reality.

Work from the outside in and then back to front.

If the cut-out characters are too thin, back them with cardboard.

A

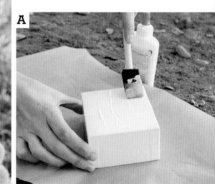

B

You'll Need

- Items to dye, such as white cotton T-shirts and pillow cases
- Elastic bands or string
- Rubber gloves
- Natural ingredients to make the dye (choose from the Dye Color Guide)
- Old sock or nylons
- White vinegar
- Salt
- Soda ash
- A large stock pot or bucket for each color
- 1 plastic bag per garment
- Baking soda (for cabbage-juice blue)

Natural Tie–Dye

Tie-dying goes back to the Egyptians, who used natural pigments to dye their fabrics. Tie-dying became popular again in the 1960s—groovy! Give an old cotton shirt a new twist with these natural tie-dyes.

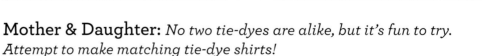

Mother & Daughter: *No two tie-dyes are alike, but it's fun to try. Attempt to make matching tie-dye shirts!*

Make It!

1. Prep your clothing. The night before, boil 4 parts water, 2 parts vinegar, 1 part salt, 1 part soda ash, and remove from the stove. Soak cotton items for up to two hours in the solution. Rinse with cold water and let dry. This will help the dye color set.

2. Prepare your dye bath. Boil a stockpot of each color you wish to use (three to four colors). Choose from the list of ingredients from the Dye Color Guide. Chop, smash, or juice ingredients. Add water and bring to a slow simmer for at least an hour; then let it cool. Strain out the ingredients and place them in an old sock or nylon, knot the end, and place it back in the pot. This way, the contents will continue to add color to your dye bath. Keep the dye bath on low heat so it is warm but not boiling.

3. Create your tie-dye design. Gather, pucker, pull, and twist sections of your garment up and secure tightly with rubber bands or string.

4. Dye your garment. Dip sections of your garment into the dye. For full coverage, submerge it. To create splatter effects, use a spray bottle. For a more controlled application, use an old condiment squeeze bottle, sponge, or paintbrush. The longer you dip, the stronger the color will be.

5. Set and cure your garment. Place the banded, dyed garment into a plastic bag and allow to sit overnight in a warm place. In the morning, rinse out your garment until the water runs clean and then hang it out to dry.

Dye Color Guide

Reds and pinks: beets, cherries, strawberries, raspberries, cranberries, pomegranate seeds, chili powder, rose petals, lavender, rosehips

Purples: red cabbage, blackberries, elderberry, grape juice, purple iris

Tans and browns: coffee grounds, tea leaves, paprika, boiled acorns

Oranges: carrot juice, yellow onion, oats

Yellows: saffron, turmeric, ginger powder, marigolds, daffodil, carrot leaves

Greens: boiled spinach, crab apples, artichokes, grass, peppermint, red onion skins

Blues: blueberries, blackberries, red cabbage (Slowly stir in baking soda, and the cabbage juice will react, creating a beautiful blue hue.)

Tip

Take your time collecting your building materials. The more variety the better!

You'll Need

- Wood glue
- Hot-glue gun and glue sticks
- Natural and recycled materials
- Twine and wire

Fairytown: Mud Brick, Bark Teepee, Stick Cabin

For centuries, girls have been building miniature houses to attract fairies and gnomes to move in and watch over their gardens and pets. Let your imagination run wild as you create a tiny dwelling using natural and recycled materials.

Mother & Daughter: *Welcome your fairy into its new home with a house warming party. Write a letter asking the fairy to watch over your garden and pets. Mom can ask the tiny guest to keep its house tidy, too!*

Make It!

1. Collect your materials. There are many wonderful places to collect your fairy building materials—in the forest, on a hike, at the park or beach, and even in your own back yard.

2. Choose a location. Fairies, like people, like to live in all sorts of different places. Pick the best place for your fairies to set up house, whether in your backyard, garden, tucked away in a tree hollow, or hidden under a deck.

3. Build the foundation. Every good house starts with a strong foundation. If you want your fairy house to be mobile, create it inside a pot, planter saucer, old bucket, on a log round, or even on an old piece of wood.

4. Create the walls. See our recipes for mud bricks, bark, or stick walls on pages 46 and 47.

5. Raise the roof. Do you want a roof that is removable so you can peek inside? Or, do you prefer a secured roof to allow your fairy some privacy? A flat roof is easy to make, while a pitched roof will give the home an old-fashioned doll house feel. Use small pieces of bark or leaves to create shingles. You can also use old recycled tin pieces cut into sheets.

6. Close the front door. A piece of scrap fabric hung in the door opening makes a nice breezy entrance. Or, create a sturdier door with a piece of bark or sticks glued together. Or, forgo the door altogether—it's up to you.

7. Decorate and accessorize. Create a pathway up to your fairy house with pebbles or crushed egg shells. Make your fairy a bench to sit and rest her weary feet. Build a fence to keep out the critters. A clothesline will allow her to dry tiny fairy clothes. And what home would be complete without a welcome sign and a mailbox to receive all your wishes?

Nature's building materials:

- Bark
- Sticks
- Moss and grass
- Leaves
- Pinecones
- Walnut shells
- Acorns
- Acorn caps
- Pebbles and small rocks
- Driftwood
- Dried flowers and lavender
- Shells
- Seaweed
- Corn husks
- Feathers
- Abandoned birds' nests
- Cattails
- Eggshells
- Beans and seeds
- Log rounds

Recycled building materials:

- Old tea pot and cups
- Recycled cans
- Bottle caps
- Sea glass (perfect for making windows)
- Old and broken pots
- Matchboxes
- Old mint tins
- Milk cartons
- Buttons and beads
- Yarn, rope, or twine
- Wooden spools
- Thimbles
- Popsicle sticks
- Toothpicks
- Wooden chopsticks
- Wine corks
- Old watch parts
- Band-Aid tin
- Clothespins
- Copper adhesive tape
- Jar lids
- Broken bits of tile
- Small jingle bells
- Marbles and old jacks
- Old tiny animal toys
- Old keys
- Paper towel or toilet paper rolls

Fairy house accessories:

- Ladder
- Swing and seesaw
- Pathway
- Clothesline
- Table and chairs
- Lantern post
- Weathervane
- Fence
- Welcome sign
- Flags
- Wishing well
- Steps
- Bench
- Bridge
- Pond
- Mailbox
- Hammock
- Outhouse

You'll Need

- 1½ pounds (680 g) of air-dry clay that you can get at your local arts and craft store

- 4 to 5 cups (1 to 1.1 kg) of dry dirt

- Grass or hay

- Water

- An old ice cube tray, or small, square or rectangle cookie cutters for shaping and drying the bricks

- A large bowl or container to mix ingredients in

Yield

This recipe makes approximately 12 to 26 bricks. The recipe is a 5:3:1 ratio.

Mud Bricks

Mud bricks make a cozy, sturdy home.

Make It!

1. Mix the soil, clay, grass, and water.

2. Continue adding soil until you achieve a cookie dough consistency.

3. Once the mixture is hand-worked through, press the mixture into the ice cube trays to form the bricks. Pop out and and set outside to dry.

4. Mud bricks take 2 to 3 days to dry, depending on the weather.

Tips

This is a messy project, so make sure to remove all of your rings and bracelets or wear some gloves when mixing and rolling.

When building the walls and laying your bricks, be sure to alternate so that the seams don't match up.

Save some of your mud mixture to use as mortar between the bricks and cracks.

Bark Teepee

Bark is the perfect material to construct the wall for a summer fairy home.

Make It!

1. Overlap slabs of bark, creating a circular round house.

2. Tie the bark with yarn or twine at the top of the house. It should look like a teepee.

Tip

Glue together the bark slabs when overlapping to create a more secure bark home for your fairy.

Stick Cabin

A stick cabin makes the perfect frontier woodland home for your pioneer fairy.

Make It!

1. Collect two sets of straight sticks: short sticks for the side walls and longer sticks for the front and back walls. The sticks should be about the same length and thickness.

2. Lay down the first two longer sticks so they are parallel.

3. Layer the second tier of shorter sticks (side walls) on top.

4. As you stack, glue or tie the corners of the sticks together with twine to secure them. Continue stacking until you reach the desired height.

5. Press the mud or clay between cracks to keep the wind out of your fairy home.

Tip

For a camouflaged and natural look, leave the sticks as is. For a lighter-colored surface, peel the bark off of your sticks.

Explore More: Spread some fairy magic in your neighborhood by inviting fairies to move into your yard, park, or even a tree down the street. Your neighbors will be surprised and enjoy the cute little homes that they find.

Summer Fairies & Garden Gnomes

Stories about fairies and gnomes have enchanted us for generations. Add a little magical fun to your day by creating your own fairies and gnomes to move into your Fairytown, tend your garden, or go on an adventure or picnic with.

You'll Need

- Paint and markers
- Paintbrush
- Scissors
- Hot glue gun and hot glue sticks
- Beads and buttons for accessories
- Other embellishments
- Lipstick or pastels

FOR FAIRIES:

- Wooden peg clothespin with flat feet (for your fairy's body)
- Chenille stems (for fairy arms)
- Clothespin base
- Scrap fabric or felt
- Yarn or ribbon
- Wings (See cutouts on pages 135 & 136.)
- Scissors or craft knife

Mother & Daughter: *Create your own fairy or gnome twin. What elements do they hold close to their hearts? Earth, fire, air, or water? Add a symbol to your fairy's wings or to your gnome's hat.*

Make it!

SUMMER FAIRIES

1. Paint the clothespin to the skin color of your choosing. Get stylish! Paint stockings on the legs of your clothespin and shoes on the base. Allow the paint to dry completely.

2. Hot glue half of a chenille stem (arms) to the back of your clothespin and trim arms to size.

3. Cut a 4" to 5" (10 to 12.5 cm) diameter circle out of fabric or felt for your fairy's dress. Make a neck hole in the middle of the circle by folding into quarters and snipping the tip off. Unfold the fabric and cut slits for the arms on either side of the neck hole. Put the dress on your fairy and tie ribbon or yarn around the waist for a belt.

4. Glue on hair and draw facial features.

5. Cut out the wings in the back of the book (page 135) or create your own wing shapes. Sew or glue the wings onto the back of the fairy.

6. Add accessories such as a necklace or wand.

Tips

Less is more with when it comes to drawing the face. Keep it simple.

Use a bit of lipstick or pastel dabbed on your finger to make her/his cheeks rosy.

Remember, if you make a mistake while drawing the face, just sand it off and start over.

Make It!
GARDEN GNOME

1. Collect several branches of different lengths that are at least 1" (2.5 cm) in diameter.

2. Cut the branches. Cut one end at an angle for the head. The other end should be flat to form a sturdy base.

3. Sand the angled end of your stick smooth so you will have a clean surface to paint your gnome's face.

4. Draw or paint your gnomes' face on the sanded, angled edge. Remember to leave room for his beard.

5. Use the wool roving or cotton balls for hair and a beard. Glue into place.

6. Create a pointy gnome hat by rolling a piece of felt around your fingers and gluing it in place.

You'll Need

FOR GNOMES:

• Several thick branches

• Wool roving or cotton balls (for hair and beard)

• Felt in assorted colors

• Handsaw

• Sandpaper

Tip
Remember, gnomes come in different shapes and sizes, just like people. Be sure to have a variety of different heights.

Nature Wands

Whirl up some magic by turning a simple stick into a Nature Wand. Nature Wands can be as simple or as intricate as you like. Remember, the most powerful wands are the ones you make with good intentions.

Mother & Daughter: *Create a wand for each kind of wish: blessing, healing, growing, playing, or any other positive thoughts. Make as many as you like because every girl should have several Nature Wands on hand for her and her friends!*

You'll Need

- A sturdy stick approximately 12" to 18" (30.5 to 46 cm) long that won't bend or break easily
- Fabric scraps, felt, or tulle
- Beads and bells
- Wire (copper or silver)
- Sea glass, gemstones, crystals, and stones
- Ribbons, trim, or tinsel
- Hot-glue gun, glue sticks and/or wood glue
- Paint and markers
- Carving knife (optional)
- Mineral oil or furniture wax
- Sandpaper

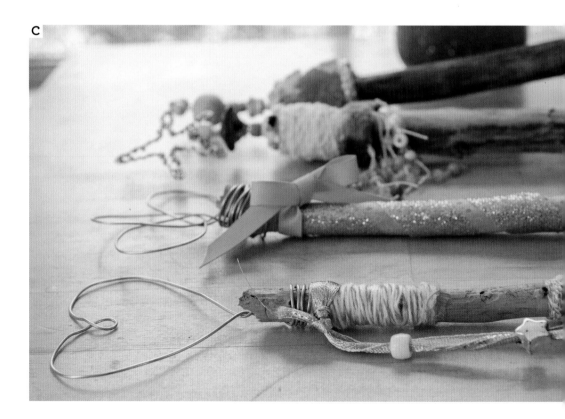

C

Make It!

1. Choose a wand branch. Choose a sturdy stick that measures at least from the crook of your arm to the tip of your middle finger—about 12" to 18" (30.5 to 46 cm). Select a stick that's comfortable to hold and refer to the "An Element for Every Season" section on page 10 to determine what type of stick has the magical properties that vibe with your personality.

2. Prepare your branch. Clean your branch and strip off the bark. Sand it until it is smooth and use a carving knife to remove knots or imperfections.

3. Decorate and construct your wand. Embellish it with wire, beads, stones, crystals, and gems. Add pictures, words, and symbols that have meaning to you. Create a handle by wrapping ribbon or fabric around the end and add streamers using ribbons or strings.

4. Polish your wand. Seal the wand with mineral oil or furniture wax to prevent it from drying out and becoming brittle (See C).

Wand Belt

Every girl with a Nature Wand needs a belt to hold this magical tool. How else are you to keep your hands free when exploring the beauty of nature? It's always a good idea to have your hands free to plant a seed and lend a hand or two.

Mother & Daughter: *Color coordinate your wand belt to a mother-daughter matching ensemble. What a fun way to play dress up and spend the day.*

You'll Need

- Felt
- Ribbon at least 1" (2.5 cm) wide (for the belt)
- Pins
- Tapestry needle and embroidery floss
- Scissors
- Accessories, such as gems, glitter, beads, or sequins
- Paper and pencil

Make It!

1. Using your wand as a guide, draw a pattern for your holster (See A).
2. Trace your pattern onto the felt and cut out.
3. Cut a 1½" (4 cm) strip of felt for the loop.
4. Prepare for sewing. Fold each piece in half. Match up the seam of the loop to the seam of the top half of the holster. Pin together for sewing.
5. Sew the seams of the holster together, making sure not to sew the top shut.
6. Embellish the belt with ribbon, beads, and gems.

A
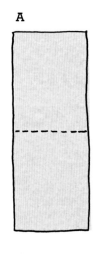
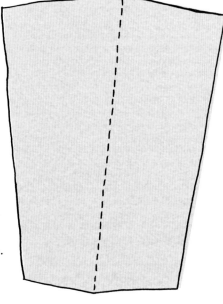

Photocopy at 200%.

Charge Your Wand for Making Wishes

What are your intentions? Close your eyes and connect and believe with your heart. Remember, some wishes take time. There is only so much your wand will be able to do, so make sure you are making the right type of wishes. Because this is a nature wand, your incantations and wishes should be nature-based.

Nature Wand Blessing

I believe in my heart
That these wishes are true.
Good spirits and healing to
me and to you.

Faith, love, and luck,
Is all that you need.
With wand in hand
Good intentions to seed.

Some good things to wish for:

• Good will
• Faith
• Happiness
• Inner peace
• Growth
• Dreams
• Confidence
• Hope
• Strength
• Healing
• Protection
• Love

The Huntress: Bow & Arrows

This elegant archery set will make any girl's heart beat faster. The bow is one of the oldest tools on earth. Crafted from simple materials, this modern take adds a bit of fun and whimsy while it embraces the strength of your girl power.

You'll Need

- Carving knife
- Sandpaper
- Mineral oil or furniture wax
- Paint and paintbrush
- Markers

FOR THE BOW:

- Deadwood tree limb at least ½" (1.3 cm) thick
- Nylon string
- Scrap fabric and yarn in various colors

FOR THE ARROWS:

- Tear-out arrow wraps (page 117)
- 3 to 6 sticks (for arrows)
- 3 to 6 wine corks (for arrowheads)
- Feathers
- Thread
- Decoupage
- Hot glue gun and glue sticks
- Craft epoxy (such as E-6000, available at craft stores)
- Scissors or craft knife

Mother & Daughter: *Every girl needs a little luck. Better your chances of scoring a bull's-eye by incorporating a good luck charm into your bow.*

Make It!

THE BOW

1. Select a piece of flexible deadwood in good condition that is about the same height as you and at least 1" (2.5 cm) thick. Try oak, lemon tree, yew, elm, or hickory. Refer to the "An Element for Every Season" section, (page 10), in the front of the book to choose a branch with magical properties.

2. Clean the branch and strip off excess bark. Use a carving knife to remove imperfections and whittle away the branch ends to make them narrower than the middle (for improved flexibility). Sand your bow, working with the natural curve. Wrap the middle of the branch with yarn and embroidery floss to create a grip.

3. String your bow. Carve bowstring notches 1" to 2" (2.5 to 5 cm) down on each branch end. Tie string into the notch at one end, then stretch the string, pulling it taught, and tie through the other notch, and then to the other end (See A, page 58).

4. Polish your bow. Seal the bow with mineral oil or furniture wax to prevent the wood from drying out and becoming brittle.

5. Wrap the ends with scraps of fabric. Add finishing touches with paint and markers.

A

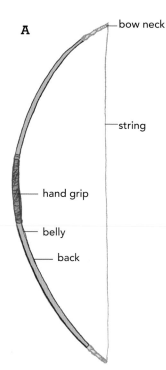

- bow neck
- string
- hand grip
- belly
- back

THE ARROWS

1. Choose straight sticks approximately ½" (1.3 cm) in diameter and half the height of the bow.

   • The best wood for arrows tends to be black locust, elm, or oak.

2. Clean your sticks and strip off the bark, using a carving knife to remove any knots or imperfections.

3. Carve a small notch at the back end of each arrow so it will sit in the bow string.

4. Cut out the paper arrow wraps on page 117. Decoupage a paper wrap around each arrow. Check the diagram for an example of placement (see B).

5. Paint stripes of various colors onto each arrow.

6. Wrap each arrow with embroidery floss to add extra textural stripes.

7. Cut a hole in the center of the cork slightly smaller than your arrow.

8. Squeeze hot glue into the hole and push the cork onto the tip of each arrow to secure.

9. Add the fletching to the arrow:

   • Cut a feather in half, cutting against the grain.

   • Space the two feather halves evenly around the ends of each arrow and glue them with epoxy.

   • Secure the feather on the arrow by wrapping thread in between the feather hairs and tying it off.

> **Tip**
>
> If you soak your corks in water for 10 minutes, they will be easier to work with and won't crumble.

B

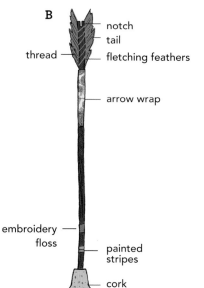

- notch
- tail
- thread
- fletching feathers
- arrow wrap
- embroidery floss
- painted stripes
- cork head

C

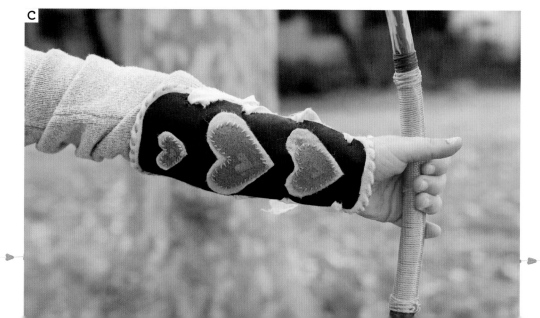

The Huntress: Arm Guard & Quiver

Give archery your best shot! These games are a fun way to build strength, endurance, and focus—but you'll need to practice, and the right equipment will set you up to win. Remember your arm guard and quiver before heading out to the range. A good archer is always prepared.

Mother & Daughter: *Bull's-eye! Take turns and see who can hit the bull's-eye first. The closest one gets a treat.*

D

The Arm Guard (See C, page 58)

Just like the days of old, protect the inside of your arm with an arm guard. Not only will yours be cute, but the protective accessory will make you look like a pro, too!

Make It!

1. Measure the length of your forearm from the inside of your elbow to your wrist.

2. Draw a pattern of your forearm on paper.

3. Pin the pattern to the felt and cut out the design and any additional felt accent shapes. We put hearts on ours.

4. Glue or sew the accent shapes to the arm guard and add further embellishments.

5. Mark four evenly spaced dots on each side of the arm guard and punch holes in those spots.

6. Lace the ribbon through the holes like you would lace up a shoe, starting at the wrist point and working your way up the forearm.

7. Put the guard on your arm and tie it snugly.

THE QUIVER (See D, above)

Draw and aim, lickity-spilt! A quiver is the perfect place to store and carry your arrows, so you're a ready shot.

Make It!

1. Make the strap by guiding the ribbon across your chest diagonally, from the top of one shoulder to the opposite hip, and around your back in the same manner until they meet. Cut the ribbon to size.

2. Using hot glue, fix the ribbon to the inside of the tube, approximately 2" (5 cm) down from the top.

3. Cover the ribbon end with duct tape to reinforce it.

4. Loosely duct tape the other ribbon end to the bottom outside of the tube to test the fit. Adjust as needed.

5. Hot glue the ribbon end to the bottom of the tube and then cover it with duct tape.

6. Decorate your tube with your scrap fabric, felt, and trim.

You'll need

FOR THE ARM GUARD:

• Felt

• Ribbon

• Paper and pencil (to create a pattern)

• Straight pins

• Scissors

• Tacky glue

• Hole punch

FOR THE QUIVER:

• Empty Pringles container or a 3" (7.5 cm) diameter cardboard cylinder shipping tube

• Scrap fabric, felt, and trim (to cover and decorate your quiver)

• 1" to 3" (2.5 to 7.5 cm) wide ribbon, approximately 36" (91.5 cm) long (for the strap)

• Hot-glue gun and glue sticks

• Duct tape

Shooting Stance

To be a successful archer, you need a comfortable, solid stance (See A).
- Stand perpendicular to the target.
- Position feet shoulder-width apart.

Loading and Shooting

- Place the notch of the arrow onto the string of your bow.
- Look at the target and raise your front bow arm to form a T.
- Pull back your string-hand to the corner of your mouth so you "kiss" the end of your arrow (See B).
- Look down the shaft of your arrow and take a deep breath.
- Focus at the target. Aim and gently set your arrow free!

Follow-Through

- Keep your bow-arm up until your arrow hits the target so your arrow arches up and away rather than down toward the ground.

A Few Safety Tips

- This game is best played with mom or dad around.
- Never point and shoot at another person. Always aim for the target.
- Stay behind the line. (Don't become the target.)

A
B

TARGET PRACTICE

Practice makes perfect. Line up and let the games begin.

Make It!

1. Tautly tie the clothesline between two trees so the string is slightly above eye level. Alternatively, tie your target directly to a tree.

2. Clothespin your paper targets to the line.

3. Mark a starting line with chalk or a rope.

4. Pour a small amount of tempera paint into paper cups (one color for each player).

5. Dip your arrow heads in the paint, aim, and shoot.

You'll Need

- Clothesline
- Clothespins
- A few sheets of large paper (to use as a targets)
- Tempera paint in various colors
- Paper cups
- Chalk or rope (for the starting line)

3

AUTUMN INTRODUCTION

Air

The autumn wind invites fall leaves to whirl about and dance. Capture these blustery moments with your special girl and with some fairy wind chimes. Explore the outdoors around you with a Nature Scavenger Hunt and hang your Punched Tin-Can Lanterns outside to light the night.

You'll Need

- Leaves and pods
- 2 heavy books
- A printing surface, such as craft paper, construction paper, tea towels, toe bags, pillowcases, etc.
- Acrylic and fabric paint
- Paintbrushes
- Brayer roller or a large spoon for burnishing

Leaf & Pod Stamping Prints

The cool autumn winds are blowing and bringing a chill to the air. Capture the spirit of the season and the natural beauty of fallen leaves with your own leaf and pod stamps. What a great, creative way to bring a touch of nature indoors!

Mother & Daughter: *Embellish reusable shopping bags with your leaf and pod stamping prints. And don't forget to show them off when you go shopping at your local farmers' market!*

Get Ready!

1. Collect a variety of leaves and pods the day before you plan to print.
2. Press the leaves in between two heavy books to flatten them overnight.

Make It!

1. Lay down some newspaper or craft paper to protect your work area.
2. Choose your canvas: You can print on a variety of surfaces, but for best results, it's wise to do a test print on paper first.
3. Using a paintbrush, add paint to the underside of the leaf or pod.
4. Carefully place the leaf or pod onto your canvas and then press it using a roller, the back of a spoon, or your hands.
5. Carefully peel the stamp off and repeat this process with your other leaves or pods.

Printing on Fabric

1. For more detailed stamps, print on tightly-woven natural fabrics like cotton or linen.
2. Remove the fabric finishes by machine washing your fabric in warm water and detergent before printing. Avoid fabric softeners or dryer sheets.
3. Press or iron the fabric and then smoothly tape it to a work surface.
4. Select acrylic-based fabric paints for stamping and check the paint label for any special instructions on heat setting.

Tips

The best leaves to use are freshly fallen so they aren't dry and brittle.

Not all leaves were made to stamp. Make sure to pick leaves that have defined veins and textures.

Glue the top of your leaf to cardboard to add extra support.

You may want to pick a few of the same kinds of leaves so you can print them in different colors.

Sprinkle glitter on your print while it's still wet to add sparkle.

When you are done using your leaf as a stamp, decorate your painted leaf with designs.

Making Rainbow Leaves

1. Squeeze out various colors of paint onto a piece of waxed paper. Four to five colors tend to work best.
2. Use your finger or a paintbrush to gently blend the edges of the paint colors together.
3. Press the leaf onto the paint so it picks up the colors and then press it on to your canvas.

Nature Scavenger Hunt: Hunting Cards

Explore your local woods, a favorite park, or a campground. Rediscover your surroundings by seeking and collecting some super-fab natural treasures! Go it alone or form teams to see who can collect the most items on the hunting card list. This is a game of hide-and-seek with a twist, so don't forget to observe, sort, and classify.

You'll Need

- A list of items to hunt for (check the Hunting List Primer for some ideas.)

- Tear-out cards from page 121

- Hole punch

- Twine or string

- A wooden bead

- Markers, colored pencils, crayons, or pastels

- Clear contact paper (optional if you'd like to laminate your cards like we did)

- Scissors or craft knife

Tip

Laminate your cards to protect them from the elements. Just sandwich your cards between two pieces of clear contact paper cut ¼" (6 mm) larger than the card along all edges.

Mother & Daughter:

Personalize your hunting gear with your name or initials. You can even arrange a mother-daughter scavenger hunt.

Hunting Cards

Hunting Cards are an easy way to remember what you are looking for, and you can reuse them. Customize your cards to fit your theme, make a few for a friend, and keep them on hand for some spur of the moment fun.

Make It!

1. Make a hunting list of 20 to 25 items. See our primer at right.

2. Cut out the nature scavenger hunt cards from the back of the book on page 121.

3. Design and color a card for each item and one for the cover.

4. Hole-punch the cards in the upper right-hand corner.

5. Thread the cards on twine or string.

6. Tie a knot in your twine and add a wooden bead or two for and accent, and you are ready to start hunting!

Hunting List Primer

- A leaf with teeth
- A fallen feather
- A dead tree
- Bark from a tree
- A bird's nest
- A seed
- An acorn
- A leaf bigger than your hand
- A stone shaped like a heart
- A Y-shaped stick
- A twig or stick shaped like the first initials of your name
- Two similar rocks
- A leaf that has insect bite marks
- An arrow head

Something that _____

- Is decaying
- Is smooth
- Is course
- Is slimy
- Is curved
- Is shiny
- Is beautiful
- Is alive
- Begins with the letter W
- Fell from a tree
- Makes noise
- A bird would eat
- Is man made
- Could be used to carry water
- An animal eats

Color Lover's Hunt

- Something blue
- Something red
- Something brown
- A purple flower
- Two different colors of moss
- A red rock
- A green four-leaf clover
- Three different colors of leaves

Listen for

- Birds chirping
- Crunching leaves
- Running water
- Animal sounds
- Wind blowing through the trees

Watch Carefully

- An ant hill
- How shadows move with the sun
- A mushroom patch
- A bug at work

Smell

- A flower
- The mud
- The fresh air
- Running water
- A pine or cedar tree
- The grass

Make & Do

- Make a leaf rubbing
- Sketch an animal or flower you saw
- String together a daisy chain crown
- Write a nature poem or story
- Make nature jewelry from your hunt treasures
- Create a wreath of leaves and branches
- Record a bird's song

Take a Picture of

- A wild animal
- A water source
- A spiderweb
- The sunset
- A hole in a tree
- Animal tracks
- A bird's egg
- A butterfly
- Animal droppings
- A beaver dam
- An animal's home

(Continued on page 69)

Nature Scavenger Hunt: Treasure Box

No scavenger hunt is complete without a treasure-filled box. Stash away all of your natural treasures in your Scavenger Hunt Treasure Box. This is a charming way to preserve all of the small objects you collect along the way.

A

You'll Need

- **A box** (shoe box)
- **Accessories** (ribbon, sequins, gems, lace, etc.)
- **Natural materials** (acorns, twigs, rocks, etc.)
- **Paint**
- **Scrap patterned paper** (pages 141 or 143)
- **Decoupage or homemade wheat paste**
- **Chipboard**
- **Pencil**
- **Scissors or craft knife**
- **Ruler**
- **Paintbrush**

Mother & Daughter: *Treasure boxes are for hiding well-guarded keepsakes and secrets. Add a lock and key to your Treasure Box.*

Make It!

1. Decorate the outside of your box by decoupaging scrap paper, ribbon, gems, and other accessories.

2. Make the inside compartments (See A). Measure the inside of the box and write down the dimensions. You will be making six compartments using chipboard to fit these dimensions.

3. Based on your dimensions, cut one strip of chipboard to fit lengthwise (on the long side). Next, cut two strips of chipboard to fit widthwise (on the small side).

4. Divide the long piece of chipboard into thirds and mark with a pencil. This is where you will cut slots.

5. Cut two slots halfway into your long piece of chipboard.

6. Divide your two smaller (widthwise) pieces of chipboard in half and mark with a pencil (for cutting slots).

7. Cut a slot halfway into each small piece of chipboard.

8. Interlock all the chipboard pieces, fitting together each notch. Place the resulting chipboard "grid" into the box.

Get Creative

- Make each compartment inside your box a different color or pattern.
- As you collect your natural treasures, arrange them by color, shape, or similarity.

A Few Extras Tools for the Hunt

- A magnifying glass for an up-close look at your findings
- Binoculars to view things that are far away or flying in the sky
- A small spray bottle with water for spritzing rocks so you can watch them change colors or spraying a spiderweb so you can see it better
- A strong magnet to drag across the dirt to determine if it contains iron (If it sticks, the answer is yes.)
- Sketchbook or travel journal to draw and write down your observations
- Sunscreen to protect you from the rays
- A water bottle to keep you hydrated

Tip

Cut cardboard slightly smaller than your measurements so the lid will fit snugly and close.

My Treasure Box

Walking Sticks

A walking stick is an incredibly valuable tool. It can be as simple or as decorative as you'd like. When hiking a trail, a walking stick will relieve stress from your knees and back and help you maintain your footing. No nature girl should enter the woods without one!

Mother & Daughter: *Choose a tree for each other. Talk about what the tree symbolizes. Why is it special? Name each other's walking stick. What does this helpful, natural walker signify for you?*

You'll Need

- A sturdy stick (that won't bend or break easily)
- Beads and bells
- Wire (copper or silver)
- Sea glass, gemstones, crystals, and mineral stones
- Ribbons, embroidery floss, trim, tinsel, feathers, and gems
- Sandpaper
- Hot-glue gun, glue sticks, and/or wood glue
- Paint and markers
- Carving knife (optional)
- Mineral oil or furniture wax

Make It!

1. Choose a straight, sturdy stick that is comfortable to hold. Consider a hard wood, such as ash, maple, oak, or birch. Remember, certain trees have magical properties! (Check the "An Element for Every Season" section on page 10).

2. Prepare your branch by cleaning it, stripping off excess bark, and sanding it until it is smooth. Use a carving knife to remove any knots or imperfections.

3. Decorate your walking stick. Embellish your walking stick with pictures, words, and symbols. Add color streamers, beads, stones, crystals, and gems. Use your imagination!

4. Polish your walking stick. Seal the stick with mineral oil or furniture wax to prevent it from drying out and getting brittle.

C

Totem Poles

Totem poles are ancient storybooks that illustrate mysterious, fascinating tales. Each totem animal is symbolic, describing traits such as loyalty, wisdom, beauty, and determination.

Mother & Daughter: *Work together and create a totem that represents your family's traits.*

You'll Need

- **4 empty cans** (any size)
- **1 large empty can with lid** (for the base)
- **Natural materials** (moss, sticks, pods, pebbles, shells, feathers, etc.)
- **Decorative accessories** (natural rope, wire, beads, sequins, and gems, etc.)
- **1 to 2 bags of beans**
- **Decoupage or homemade wheat paste**
- **Colored and decorative papers** (See tear-outs pages 141 & 143)
- **Charcoal pencil**
- **Hot-glue gun and glue sticks**
- **Scissors**
- **Acrylic paints**
- **Paintbrushes**
- **Pastels**

Make It!

1. Paint all cans with a basecoat of white acrylic paint to create a clean canvas for your totem pole.

2. Use acrylic paints to coat each can in a different color. Consider colors that represent the elements. For example, use green for the earth.

3. Measure and cut five pieces of paper to wrap around each can like a label (See A).

4. Choose the five animals that best represent you. Ideally, you should pick at least one from each element (See page 10). Decide on the stacking order and then draw and cut out your animals on the paper (See B).

5. Paint the animals. Using a charcoal pencil to create black outlines and pastels for shading.

6. When you're happy with your animal, decoupage it to the can (See C).

7. Fill the base can with beans to keep the totem pole upright and steady (See D). Hot glue the lid closed.

8. Stack your cans in order and hot glue the seams together to form a seal (See E).

9. Decorate and add the finishing touches.

A

B

D

What Are Your Animal Totems?

What would a totem pole say about your personality? While making your own version, choose animal traits that have the most meaning to you. Check the "An Element for Every Season" on page 10 for some clues.

Time to Decorate! Breathe life into your animals with the natural materials you collected. Cover the seams between the cans. Use moss for hair or add a sequin or two to make your totem shine in the sun. Embellish the eyes with some beads. Add wings to one of your animals so it can take flight.

Scale Down: Instead of using cans, you can do the same project on a smaller scale using toilet paper or paper towel cardboard tubes.

E

You'll Need

- A branch 16" to 20" (41 to 51 cm) long

- Paint

- Yarn, string, or ribbon

- Beads

- Bells

- **Found objects** (old keys, buttons, bottle caps, bells, etc.)

- **Natural materials** (pinecones, acorns, shells, driftwood, sticks, feathers, etc.)

- **Salt dough clay** (recipe on page 89)

- **Leaves** (for making imprints)

- **A straw or chopstick** (for poking holes into the top of the leaf chimes)

- Knife

- Rolling pin

Fairy Wind Chimes

As the weather starts to cool, invite fairies to make music for you with a set of fairy wind chimes. Wind chimes are thought to be a source of good luck and positivity. Every time you hear a chime clanging in the breeze, a bit of good luck, peace, and harmony is headed your way.

Mother & Daughter: *Pick out a good luck charm and a lucky note for each other's wind chime.*

Make It!

1. Gather found and natural materials; then select a sturdy branch to use as the chime base.

2. Paint and decorate the branch; then set aside to dry.

3. String the objects and tie them to the branch, hanging the heaviest object in the middle of the branch to act as a pendulum.

MAKE CLAY LEAF CHIMES

1. Roll out salt dough approximately ¼" (6 mm) thick.

2. Press a leaf into the clay, vein side down, or make your own leaf-shaped design like we did.

3. Cut around the leaf, and poke a hole for hanging.

4. Allow the clay to dry. When the leaf chimes are dry, they are ready to string and hang. You can leave them their natural color or paint them.

Hang Your Wind Chimes

Traditionally, wind chimes are hung outside on a porch or balcony, but you can hang your fairy wind chimes anywhere the wind may catch them so you can hear them blowing in the breeze.

Tip

Vary the length of the strands that hold objects to add interest.

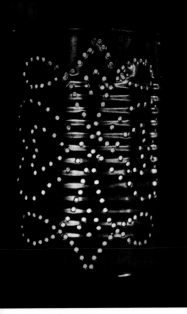

Punched Tin-Can Lanterns

Celebrate autumn with the festive candlelight glow of a punched tin-can lantern. In the olden days, candles were the only source of light. Pierced lanterns were used to protect the flame from blowing out when one had to trek from the home to the outhouse. Today, these luminaries are the perfect centerpieces to softly light your autumn table when your love ones gather. Use them to light a path to your door, hang them from a tree, or display them in your yard or window.

You'll Need

- Clean, empty tin cans (You can use any size.)
- Votive candles
- Hammer
- An assortment of nails in different sizes (for larger and smaller holes)
- Tear-out stencil patterns, (page 127), or paper and pencil to make your own
- Masking tape
- Scissors or craft knife
- Wire hanger
- Wire cutters
- Towel
- Sand

Mother & Daughter: *Just like leaves, no two lanterns are alike. Design your own unique patterns, but choose a theme so your lanterns coordinate.*

Prep Work

1. The day before you make this project, remove any labels on the cans.
2. Fill each can with water and freeze overnight until solid. The ice will support the can and prevent it from denting when you punch holes through it.

Make It!

1. Choose a pattern. We provided a few stencils of our favorite designs in the back of the book on page 127. Or, you can draw your own.
2. Tape your stencil to the can. Prevent the can from moving by cradling it in a folded towel.
3. Gently tap a nail into the pattern using a hammer until the nail has punched through. Repeat until you finish punching out the pattern.

Tip

Stay away from cans that once held flammable materials or old paint.

4. Once you have completed punching the pattern, rinse the can in warm water so the ice melts. Then allow the lantern to dry.

5. Consider jazzing up your lanterns by painting them coordinating colors or adding a bit of glitter and a bit of sparkle. Use rust-resistant paint if you are going to use your lanterns outside.

TO MAKE THE HANDLES

1. To hang your lantern, punch a hole on each side of the lantern rim. With your wire cutters, cut out 18" to 21" (46 to 53.5 cm) of wire from your hanger. Bend and arch the wire in half and insert each end into a hole. Crimp and bend the ends up to secure them. Place 1" to 2" (2.5 to 5 cm) of sand in the bottom of the lantern to give it some weight. Press a candle into the sand so that it will stay in place. Light your candle.

Lanterns Year-Round: In the summer, use your lanterns as insect repellent by placing citronella candles in them to keep the bugs away.

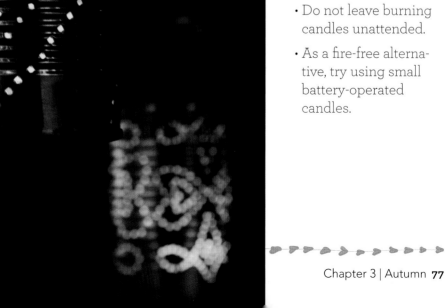

Draw Your Own Pattern

- Measure and cut a piece of paper that wraps around each can (like a label).
- Draw your pattern on the paper.
- Simple, easy, recognizable designs tend to work best. Think starbursts, diamonds, and circles. Folk art, knitting, and embroidery patterns are a great source of inspiration!
- The punched hole will be larger than your hand-drawn dot, so be sure to leave enough space between dots.

Fire Safety Tips

- Place the lanterns on a fire-safe surface (they get hot!).
- Do not leave burning candles unattended.
- As a fire-free alternative, try using small battery-operated candles.

Wind Sock Chandelier

Wind socks were originally intended to be used as a tool to tell the direction and force of the wind, but why not use them to add a bit of elegance and whimsy to your garden, front porch, or even inside a window? Transform your space and provide a magical aura with these handmade wind socks.

Mother & Daughter: *Write or embroider hidden messages on each strip to carry your good thoughts and feelings into the breeze.*

You'll Need

- **12" (30.5 cm) hoop** (a quilter's hoop, brass ring, embroidery hoop, or if you are feeling super crafty, upcycle an old lampshade frame)
- **Ribbon**
- **A variety of fabric torn into strips**
- **Trim, yarn, lace, and pom-poms** (pretty much anything you want to hang)
- **String, twine, or fishing line for hanging**
- **Lobster clasp with a swivel** (so when the windsock spins in the wind it won't get tangled)
- **Scissors**
- **Pencil**

Make It!

1. Make streamers by tearing strips of fabric in various widths, ½" to 2" (1.3 to 5 cm) long.

2. Create the frame by dividing your hoop into four quarters. Mark each with a pencil to denote where you will attach the strands to hang your windsock chandelier.

3. Use strips of fabric to make four even braids.

4. Attach each braided strand to a quarter mark on your hoop.

5. Gather and knot together all four braided strands.

6. Thread your fishing line through the knot and tie it to the lobster clamp.

7. Attach the streamers by tying and knotting ribbon and fabric strips to the hoop.

8. Hang your windsock chandelier on a post or up high where it can catch the breeze.

Tips

Experiment with different lengths of ribbons.

Add bells or beads at the end of your ribbons to hear a pleasing sound as they blow in the breeze.

Create texture by adding loose stitching in the center of some streamers. Use embroidery thread and gather up the streamers before tying a knot.

Explore More:

Create a garland around the top of your hoop with jasmine and lavender to add a bit of fragrance to the air as it swings in the breeze. Or, add some Christmas lights for that extra bit of twinkle at night.

Tip

Brush up on the rules with a quick online lesson at www.domino-games.com/domino-rules.

You'll Need

- Rocks
- Decoupage paste or homemade wheat paste
- Paintbrush
- Tear-outs (pages 123 & 125)
- Markers
- Glitter
- Stamps
- Paint
- Decorative accents
- **4 sticks** (for tic-tac-toe)
- Scissors or craft knife

Rock Games

Just like stone soup, you can make a lot out of almost nothing at all. These games require gathering just a few simple items. So grab your favorite markers, stamps, stickers, paint, a bit of decoupage, and your imagination and let the games begin.

Mother & Daughter: *You can make these quick and easy projects and you'll have a fun game in no time. They're perfect for family gatherings, camping trips, and rainy days.*

The first step to playing any rock games is to collect your stones. You can collect them from just about anywhere: on a hike, at the beach, or even in your own backyard. Flat, smooth stones tend to work best for these games.

MEMORY MATCH-UP

This is a twist on the classic match-up game of memory. You'll need 12 to 16 stones (an even number).

Make It! Cut out two of each icon from the tear-outs on pages 123 and 125, and adhere them to the stones with decoupage paste. Apply the decoupage on the back and top of each icon. Each stone will need at least two coats to be fully sealed. If you're feeling extra creative, customize your stones by using your own photographs as the characters. Just remember, you'll need two (one pair) of each icon to play this game.

STORY STARTERS

These stones will flex your storytelling muscles while kick-starting your imagination. What story will you tell?

Make It! You make these the same way you made the Memory Match-Up Stones. In fact, you can reuse some of the same stones, just be sure to remove any doubles. Include an even number of rocks from each category: people, animals, objects and props, places, and actions and obstacles. Get some ideas from the list at right!

TIC-TAC-TOE

Who says you need Xs and Os? You can use any icon you'd like from hearts and ladybugs to suns and moons.

Make It! For this game you'll need ten rocks: five of each icon for each player. Make the game board by tying together some sticks or painting the board on a satchel, using it as your portable game board and a place to store your stones.

DOMINOES

You will need a total of twenty-eight rocks to make a full set of dominos.

Make It! Paint or use a marker to make a horizontal line across the center of the rock. Paint two sets of dots from zero to six: one for each side of the dividing line.

Story Starters: Some Ideas to Get You Off on the Right Track

People: queens, kings, princesses, princes, witches, mermaids, fairies,

Animals: frogs, ladybugs, horses, birds, dogs, owls, lions, elephants, mice, dragons

Objects and props: hats, keys, wands, baskets, candles, sailboats, pumpkins, cupcakes, magnifying glass, flashlight, flowers

Places: castles, forest, daytime (sun), nighttime (moon and stars), farm, dungeon, tent, tee-pee, hot-air balloon

Actions and Obstacles: rain clouds, locked doors, bridge, a letter, lightbulb (idea), a broken vase, map, a black cat, do-not-enter sign, a bee sting, caldron

To Play

Use as few as ten and up to thirty-six stones, but remember that the more stones you have, the more exciting the story becomes. Each stone takes the story in a new direction. Start your story by placing the stones face down and picking one at random. When you come to a stopping point, turn over the next stone and begin weaving the elements of the story together. There's no wrong way to play—you can play alone or with a big group.

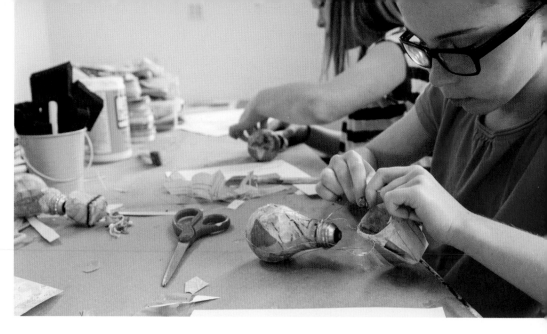

Lightbulb Hot-Air Balloon Ornament

Did you know that the hot-air balloon is the oldest and most successful human-flight carrier? Hot air balloons do a whole lot more than just carry us around. They are a reminder that things are looking up and improving every day. Good luck and health are on the way!

Take something old and make it new. By reusing materials in a different way, you get to breathe new life into something that would normally get tossed in the trash. Plus, you will earn some extra karma points from Mother Earth for practicing upcycling.

Mother & Daughter: *Uplift someone's spirits by adding small pieces of paper with your written words of encouragement decoupaged onto your lightbulb balloon.*

You'll Need

- An old lightbulb
- Tissue paper, old clothing, pattern paper, or scrap paper
- Decoupage or homemade wheat paste
- Paintbrush or foam brush
- Thin-gauge wire
- Wire cutters or nail clippers
- Origami paper tear-outs and origami instructions (pages 129–130)
- A safety pin
- Painter's tape
- Scissors or craft knife
- Decorative accessories (string, embroidery floss, beads, sequins, gems, etc.)

Selecting Paper

Thin tissue paper or paper that has a similar weight works best for this project—old sewing patterns, recycle patterned napkins, or gift-wrapping tissue.

Tissue paper is easy to wrap and form around the lightbulb's curved surface and will layer nicely, as lines and textures from previous layers will show through. Pre-cut your tissue paper or tear it into narrow strips for a soft effect.

Make It!

1. Decoupage your lightbulb with tissue paper. Apply decoupage or home-made wheat paste with a paintbrush and allow to dry completely.

2. Fold your balloon basket. Use the origami paper tear-outs on pages 129–130 and directions on how to fold the basket.

3. Brush a coat of decoupage or wheat paste on the basket and allow it to dry. This helps seal the folds and creates a lacquered look.

4. To hang the basket, cut two even pieces of wire (about 15" [38 cm] long), enough to wrap around the top of the light bulb and attach to the basket.

5. Cut a third piece of wire (about 10" [25 cm] long) to wrap around the metal base of the lightbulb.

6. Use the safety pin to create four pinholes in each corner of the basket to thread and tie off the wire.

7. Form the two long wires into an X by crisscrossing them and twisting the wires in the center (See A).

8. Center the X on top of the lightbulb and bend the wires down toward the base. Use painter's tape to hold the wire in place as you form and twist it.

9. Take the third wire and wrap it around the metal base once. Loop the two long wires into place over the third base wire. Then, wrap the third base wire around again once or twice to secure all wires, twisting the ends to finish (See B).

10. Next, thread each longer wire through the basket hole you created and twist it back up to secure (See C).

11. Add a ribbon to the top of your lightbulb balloon to hang it, a decorative accessory around the metal base, and a tail to the basket. Add a few gems and glitter for extra sparkle.

Tips

Pick up tissue paper pieces by using the tip of a wet paintbrush.

Avoid getting the tissue paper too wet or it will disintegrate.

Use a narrow-necked bottle to keep your lightbulb in place while you are decoupaging. This will also work as a drying stand.

Create a mobile by making more than one of these ornaments.

A

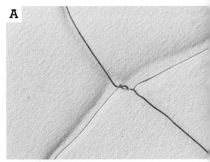

B

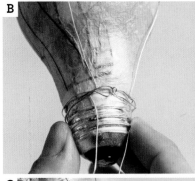

C

WINTER INTRODUCTION

4 Water

It's that time of the year for us girls to cozy up and stay warm as the snow flutters down to the ground. But that doesn't mean we can't create some fantastic crafts, too! What a great time for us to think of the fun we had all year and store them in a Happy Thoughts Jar, or make some crafty gifts like brooches, salt dough bowls, or Peaceful Mind Globes.

You'll Need

- Medallion cut-outs (pages 119 &121)
- Wood circular discs 1" to 2" (2.5 to 5 cm) in diameter
- Felt in assorted colors
- Ribbons (at least 1" [2.5 cm] wide)
- Jewelry pin back bar
- Pinking shears and scissors
- Needle and thread
- Hot-glue gun and glue sticks
- Decoupage or homemade wheat paste
- Markers, colored pencils, and pastels
- Paint and paintbrush
- Scissors or craft knife
- Additional accessories (gems, glitter, sequins, etc.)

FOR THE BADGE:

- 4" (10 cm) piece of medium gauge wire

Badge & Ribbon Medallions

Every now and then, we all need a pat on the back. Show off your own accomplishments or congratulate someone for their's with these badges and ribbon medallions. What better way to express your achievements and gratitude?

Mother & Daughter: *Stage an award ceremony. What categories will you create? Some ideas include best picker-upper, longest napper, and best dressed. Are there any other top honors?*

Make It!

1. Cut out a medallion of your choice (see pages 119 and 121).
2. Color the medallions with markers, colored pencils, and paint.
3. Attach the medallion to the top of the circular wood disc using decoupage or wheat paste.
4. Allow the medallion dry completely.

BADGE OF HONOR (See A)

1. Cut a piece of ribbon or felt 6" (15 cm) long and at least 1" (2.5 cm) wide.
2. Create a point on each end of the ribbon by folding the corners down to form a triangle point and glue as shown.
3. Make a small figure eight with your wire to attach the wooden medallion to the ribbon (See C).
4. Hot glue one loop of the figure eight to the back of the medallion (See D).
5. Fold the ribbon in half, sandwiching the other loop of the figure eight in between the two triangle points; glue them together (See E).
6. Add bling with gems, glitter, and sequins.
7. Glue or stitch the pin back bar to the top back of your ribbon (See F).

AWARD RIBBON (See B)

1. Cut a piece of ribbon or felt that is 4" (10 cm) long and at least 1" (2.5 cm) wide. This will be your base ribbon.
2. Snip the corners off each end of the ribbon to form a V shape.
3. Layer thinner additional felt ribbons on top of this base ribbon.
4. Use your wooden disc as a pattern to cut out two circle shapes. You will sandwich the ribbons between these circles. Cut out smaller circles with pinking shears or regular scissors to complete the look.
5. Finish by gluing all the pieces together, adding the bling, gems, glitter, or sequins and fastening the pin back bar to the back of the ribbon with glue or stitching.

Words and phrases to include on your medallions:

• Explorer	• Social butterfly	• Being brave	• Clever fox	• Hope
• Readiness medal	• Sharing is caring	• Girl power	• Love bug	• Love
• Handy helper	• I'm fearless	• Just us girls	• Nature princess	• Happiness
• Savvy crafter	• Being brave	• Positive power	• Best friends	• Smile
	• Pixie power	• Bouncing bunny	• Friendship	• I am enough

C

D

E

F

You'll Need

FOR THE DOUGH:

- A bowl

- 1 cup (288 g) salt

- 2 cups (125 g) all-purpose flour

- 1 cup (235 ml) lukewarm water

- 1 tablespoon (5 ml) **vegetable oil** (to make the dough easier to knead)

- 1 tablespoon (5 ml) **lemon juice** (to make the finished product harder)

CREATION TOOLS AND MATERIALS:

- Acrylic paint

- A rolling pin

- **A straw, skewer, chopstick, or toothpick** (for poking holes in the top of pendants, ornaments, chimes, and jewelry)

- **Cookie cutters, bottle caps, and cups** (to create basic shapes)

- **Bowls and molds** (for pressing in dough)

- **Stamps, leaves, shells, and objects** (for adding texture and making dough impressions)

- **Pizza cutter** (for cutting straight lines and strips)

- **Safety pins or jewelry pin back bars** (for creating broaches)

- **Magnetic strips** (for creating magnets)

- **Ribbon, string, yarn** (for creating ornaments and pendants)

- Markers

- Glue

- Glitter

Salt Dough Crafts

This is a perfect way to pass a wintery day indoors. Let your imagination go wild by creating salt dough crafts! You can create magnets, ornaments, paperweights, jewelry, bowls, trinket dishes, and more. Salt dough is an easy, natural form of pottery—and you can do it all in your own kitchen.

Mother & Daughter: *Salt Dough Monogrammed Pendants are a perfect way to customize and personalize any creation.*

Make It!
MAKE THE DOUGH

1. Mix the flour, salt, vegetable oil, and lemon juice in bowl.

2. Gradually stir in water for a doughy consistency.

3. Form the dough into a ball and knead for about 5 minutes until dough is smooth and elastic.

4. Now the salt dough is ready to be worked into any shape you desire.

DRYING YOUR CREATIONS

Allow the salt dough to air dry, or bake it in the oven at 200° F (93 C°) until the dough is dry.

BAKE TIME: This will depend on the size and thickness of your creations.

- Thin, flat ornaments can take 45 to 60 minutes.

- Thicker creations can take 2 to 3 hours or more.

- Allow creations to cool before you begin decorating.

ADD SOME COLOR

Add food coloring or mix in natural pigments using cinnamon, coffee grounds, cocoa, paprika, curry powder, or powdered tempera paints. Make several colorful batches of dough in different colors.

Tips

Dust some flour on your hands and sprinkle on your work area to prevent dough from sticking.

Store your unused salt dough in an airtight container in the refrigerator for up to one week.

If you are going to bake your creations in the oven until they are dry, check on them periodically and rotate them to make sure both sides dry and they don't brown.

Creative Possibilities

- Pendants
- Chimes
- Broaches
- Magnets
- Paperweights
- Beads and jewelry
- Bowls and trinket dishes
- Holiday ornaments
- Picture frames
- Plaques
- Wreaths
- Coil vases

Woodland Animal Masks

Let your inner animal run wild! Try on these Woodland Animal Masks and explore your courage, wit, and speed.

Mother & Daughter: *Use your imagination and make up games to go with your masks. Play a game of animal hide-and-seek, or put on a play and act as your woodland animal character.*

You'll Need

- Tear-out animal patterns (pages 130–131)
- Various colored felt and scrap fabric
- Accents (fabric paint, glitter, gems, pom-poms, feathers, sequins)
- Scissors or craft knifes
- Embroidery thread
- Tapestry needle
- Fabric paint
- Fabric glue
- Ribbon or elastic
- Straight pins

Make it!

1. Choose a woodland animal. (See the opposite page for help.)

2. Use the patterns on pages 130–131 to select a basic mask shape.

3. Choose felt and fabric colors—you can use traditional or nontraditional colors.

4. Pin the pattern onto felt or fabric and cut out the basic shape. (You'll need to cut two—one for the outside and one as a liner).

5. Glue or sew your pieces together, layering the inside color of the ears, and adding the nose and eye circles.

6. Embellish the masks with paint, glitter, embroidery, gems, or feathers.

7. Sandwich ribbon between the inner liner and the outside of the mask at your temple line and attach the ribbon by sewing or gluing. These ribbons will tie around the back of your head.

8. Glue the front and inside-liner shapes together. (The liner hides any interior sewing.)

9. Put your mask on and you are ready to play.

Woodland power animals to consider making

Bunny: shy, fast, creative, family-oriented
Owl: wise, mysterious, intelligent, protector
Bear: brave, courageous, confident, nurturing
Fox: quick-witted, adaptable, clever, strategic
Deer: loving, graceful, swift, beautiful, creative
Coyote: resourceful, playful, intelligent, enthusiastic
Raccoon: bright, clever, mischievous
Skunk: confident, aware, good judgment
Butterfly: represents resurrection, transition, celebration, lightness
Hedgehog: cool and calm, intuitive, resourceful, intelligent
Wolf: intelligent, cunning, friendly, compassionate

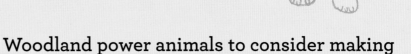

Happy Thoughts Jar

Collect and hold onto your happy thoughts so you can refresh your memory with these joyful messages time and again. Use your jar to collect small mementos and trinkets that have personal meaning to you. Write down small positive moments that happened during the day on a piece of paper and drop them into the jar. When you are feeling blue, just reach into the jar and pull out a few happy thoughts to cheer you up.

You'll Need

- A large jar
- Trinkets and memorabilia
- Approximately 365 strips of paper for writing down your happy thoughts (Use the pattern paper tear-outs from the back of the book on pages 139 & 141.)
- Tissue paper
- Gems, glitter, yarn
- Decoupage or homemade wheat paste
- Jar label tear-outs (page 113)
- Scissors or craft knife

Mother & Daughter: *Make this an annual tradition. At the start of every year, make a new Happy Thoughts Jar. When the year comes to a close, pull out all of the happy thoughts and read and reflect on them together.*

Make It!

1. Pick a jar large enough to hold a year's worth of mementos and strips of paper.

2. Decorate and decoupage the outside of the jar and lid with tissue paper, gems, and glitter. Don't forget to inscribe the year on the label.

3. Start off the jar by adding trinkets and memorabilia that represent what you want to invite into your life, house, and home. See the list on the opposite page for inspiration.

4. Add strips of paper and mementos that represent your happy thoughts, goals, and hopes for the upcoming year.

5. Be sure to put your Happy Thoughts Jar in a place where you will see it on a daily basis.

6. Make adding to your Happy Thoughts Jar part of your daily routine. This will keep you in the happy zone!

2015

happy Thoughts jar

Memorabilia and trinkets to consider:

Feathers: to symbolize freedom

Keys: to keep or unlock secrets, provide access

Flowers: to represent beauty, growth, and positive thoughts

Song lyrics: your favorite song or music notes

Acorn: to symbolize protection, prosperity, and power

Pinecone: a symbol of nature and life

Shells: a reminder of the beach, happiness, and good news

Roots: to represent family, to feel grounded

Quartz: for clarity

Rose petals: for love

Needle and thread: to sew, create, and mend broken ties

Silver dollar: for wealth and to represent spending money wisely

Paintbrush: to represent creativity

Four-leaf clover: for luck

Stars: as promise of success

Butterfly: to symbolize transition

Heart: for love

Bicycle charm: if you want to learn to ride a bike

Bottle cap: as a reminder of a shared drink

Candy wrapper: as reminder of something sweet

A favorite recipe: a reminder of home and homemade treats

Quote or a poem: to be insightful

Ticket stub: to remember your favorite movie

You'll Need

- 5 toothpicks per doll
- 2 to 4 packets of embroidery floss (1 flesh color, 1 shirt color, 1 color for the skirt/pants, and 1 hair color)
- Small wooden bead for the head
- Hot-glue gun and glue sticks
- Tacky glue
- Scissors
- Markers and pastels to draw the face
- Scrap fabric, ribbon, yarn, trim, buttons, and sequins to personalize and dress up your dolls

Don't You Worry Doll

Tell your fears to go away by sharing them with your Don't You Worry Doll. These uplifting dolls originated in Guatemala and are said to carry your troubles and fears away as you sleep. They traditionally come in sets of six. Tell your doll your troubles and place her under your pillow while you sleep. Each Worry Doll will carry your fears away so you start each day refreshed and upbeat.

Mother & Daughter: *Create a comfy spot for your dolls to sleep in a small cloth bag or box by your bedside.*

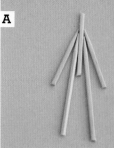

A

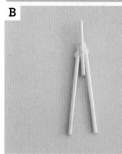

B

Make It!

1. Trim and arrange your toothpicks (See A).

   • 2 toothpicks for the legs

   • 2 trimmed toothpicks for the arms, approximately 1" (2.5 cm) long

   • 1 trimmed toothpick for the torso, approximately 1" to 1½" (2.5 to 4 cm) long

2. Hot glue the legs to the torso. The toothpick points should be positioned at the halfway mark on the torso toothpick (See B).

3. Using the pants- or skirt-colored embroidery floss, start halfway down the torso and floss around the body and legs of the worry doll. Wrap the legs individually or together (if you want to make a skirt). Just don't wrap the legs all the way down so there is room for the feet (See C).

4. Hot glue on the arms. The flat part of the toothpick will be the hand and the pointed will be the shoulder. Glue the shoulder to the torso midway up the body (See D).

5. With your shirt-colored floss, wrap each arm individually, leaving a bit of toothpick showing on each end. Decide whether your doll will wear short or long sleeves (See E). Wrap more floss around the shoulders to cover up the hot glue and points of the sticks. Wrap under the arms and around the body to form the rest of the shirt and glue down the floss with tacky glue.

6. Hot glue the bead to the "neck" for the head.

7. Cover the bead with tacky glue and wrap the head with your flesh-colored floss (See F).

8. Draw the face on top of the floss. (You can also choose to leave the face blank.)

9. Glue on the hair.

10. Add extra details to personalize and accessorize your doll using scrap fabric, ribbon, yarn, sequins, buttons, and trim.

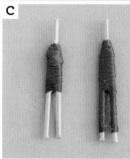

C

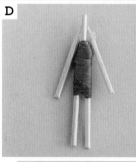

D

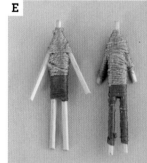

E

F

K

You'll Need

- **Stickers** (of course!)

- At least 1 piece of 8½" × 11" (22 × 28 cm) **release paper** (You can find this at your local craft store, or reuse the backing paper from a sheet of address labels like we did.)

- 1 piece of 8½" × 11" (22 × 28 cm) **heavy card stock for the cover** (You may also want to use the patterned paper supplied in the back of the book on pages 141 or 143 for your cover.)

- **Colorful tape** (such as washi tape)

- **Stapler**

- **Clear contact paper** (optional, if you'd like to laminate your cover)

- **Embroidery floss**

- **Scissors**

- **A button or bead**

- **Glue stick**

- **Tapestry needle**

- **Pens and markers**

Pocket Sticker Book

Create a place where you can store, trade, and gift your cutest and most sparkly stickers! This Pocket Sticker Book is a great way to imagine scenes and stories and show off and share your fabulous sticker collection!

Tip

To thicken up your book, fold and sew in additional pieces of release paper in the middle of your book.

Mother & Daughter: *Dedicate a page to you and your mom. Where will you go? What exciting adventures will you have?*

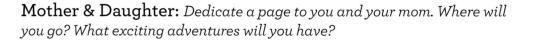

Make It!

1. Collect all of your favorite stickers and don't forget those cute little stickers that come on fruit, address labels, and postage stamps. Stickers are everywhere!

2. Fold your release paper to make the inside pages.

   - Fold the paper in half horizontally (See A).

   - Fold in half again (See B).

   - And then fold in half again (See C).

   - Unfold and you will have eight rectangles (See D).

   - Fold the "book" in half and cut from the fold to the first crease (See E and F).

   - Fold over in opposite directions (See G).

   - Fold in half vertically and again horizontally to finish making the inside pages (See H).

3. Staple together the open seams at the sides and bottom of the doubled pages, and cover the staples with colorful tape to form pockets to store extra stickers and scraps of paper (See I).

4. Cut and fold your cover card stock so it is ¼" (6 mm) larger than your inside book pages.

5. Customize your book by drawing on and decorating the front. Don't forget to write the author's name (yours) or "My Sticker Book" on the cover.

6. Protect the cover by laminating it between two pieces of clear contact paper that are a ¼" (6 mm) larger than your card stock cover.

7. Arrange all of your pages together. Place the cover on the bottom and then stack the interior release pages (opened) on top.

8. With your embroidery floss and needle, stitch your cover and interior pages together at the fold in the middle from the bottom up. Then tie a knot and extend the floss to make a bookmark. Add a few beads at the end (See J).

9. To make the clasp, sew a loop on the back cover and a button or bead on the front cover and then start adding your favorite stickers (See K).

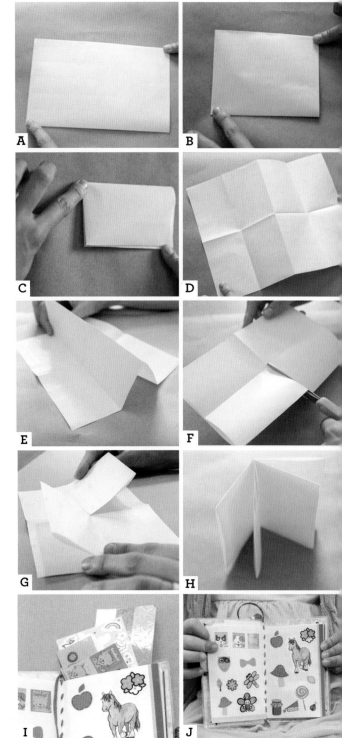

A

B

C

D

E

F

G

H

I

J

You'll Need

- 2 flesh-colored chenille stems 12" (30.5 cm) long
- 2 packets of embroidery floss (1 flesh-colored and 1 stocking-colored)
- 3/8" to 3/4" (1 to 2 cm) wooden bead for the head
- Decorative accessories (ribbon, yarn, embroidery floss, beads, sequins, gems, and scrap fabric)
- Yarn, raffia, burlap twine, or wool roving
- Lavender or other dried flowers
- Natural materials (acorn tops, moss, and leaves)
- Cotton balls
- Tapestry needle and thread
- Red and black waterproof ink pens
- Mint tin or small box
- White glue
- Hot-glue gun and glue sticks

Tiny Lavender Flower Doll & Bed

This tiny flower doll is a modern take on an old-fashioned craft that has been enjoyed for generations. This sweet doll is a dreamy companion in her bed, and she's just the right size to fit into your jacket pocket or to tuck away in a drawer.

Mother & Daughter: *Bring out your creative whimsy by inviting your mother–daughter friends over to make a flower doll for each season.*

Make It!

ARM AND TORSO

1. Fold one chenille stem in half (See A, left).

2. Twist the top ¼" (6 mm) of the chenille stem together to form the neck (See A, middle).

3. Fold the ends of the chenille stem inward toward the center and down to form the arms and torso. Form a T—the arms should be about 1¾" (4.4 cm) long and longer than the torso (See A, right).

LEGS

1. Fold the chenille stem in half (See B, left).

2. Fold the ends back and toward the center (See B, middle).

3. Tightly twist the chenille stems to connect the torso to the leg section (See B, right).

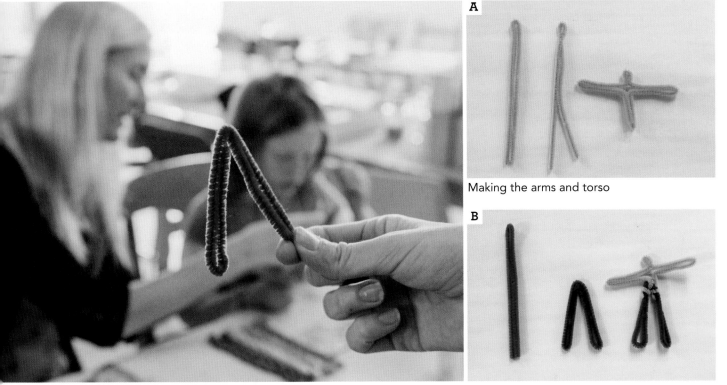

Making the legs

A

Making the arms and torso

B

Combining the legs and torso

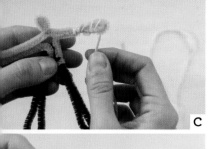
C

D

E

F

G

H

WRAPPING THE DOLL

1. Thread a tapestry needle with a 4" to 5" (10 to 13 cm) length of the flesh-colored floss so the thread is doubled, but do NOT tie a knot. You'll start with the unknotted end of the floss to wrap your doll.

2. Begin in the middle of one arm. Spiral-wrap the floss around the arm until you get to the hand loop (See C).

3. Thread the tapestry needle around and through the chenille stem loop, covering it completely (See D and E). You are done using the tapestry needle until it is time to finish off the floss.

4. Wrap the floss back over the hand covering the loop and continue to wrap the arm, working your way in toward the torso. Make sure the thread lays flat and does not get twisted. Crisscross around the torso and continue on to the next arm (See F).

5. Finish off the wrapping by threading the needle under the already-wrapped floss to secure it (See G). Cut the needle off and trim the remaining threads.

6. Wrap the torso and legs in the same way.

7. When you are finished wrapping your doll, bend the chenille stem at the end of the arms and legs to form hands and feet (See H).

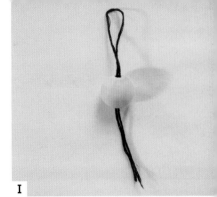

I

Tip

If you run out of floss, finish off the strand and re-thread a new piece of floss. Simply overlap it with the old and continue to wrap the doll.

M

J

MAKING THE FACE AND HAIR

1. Choose your doll hair thread/yarn and gather it.

2. Cut a piece of embroidery floss about 5" (13 cm) long.

3. Fold the floss in half and thread it through the wooden head bead, leaving a loop at the top (See I).

4. Put the hair through the loop, pull the ends until tight, and then secure (See J).

5. Squeeze hot glue into the bead hole. Fit the wooden bead on the neck (See K).

6. Trim your doll's hair to the desired length.

7. Draw facial features on the bead with an ink pen or marker. Keep it simple. Use a bit of lipstick dabbed on your finger to make her cheeks rosy. If you make a mistake, just sand it off and start over.

8. Dress your tiny doll by hot gluing several layers of dried lavender and flowers to form a full skirt. Wrap with burlap or string to form a waistband, hiding the glued ends (See L).

9. Accessorize by adding a belt, crown, necklace, or even a pair of fairy wings and a magic wand. Add a few small buttons and gems to finish her outfit.

10. Use paint, paper, scrap fabric, and trim to decorate the tiny tin that will become her bed. Make a pillow with fabric and fill with a cotton ball or two to add some fluff. Sew up a quilt and add a tiny tulle skirt to her bed for frills (See M).

K

L

You'll Need

- **Map pins** (found at your local office supply store)
- **4 pieces of thick cardboard** (cut to the same size, without any creases)
- **Acrylic paint and paintbrushes**
- **A thick ribbon** (wide and long enough to wrap around the edge of your cardboard)
- **Scrap paper to use as your template**
- **Scissors**
- **Pencil**
- **Painter's tape**
- **Embroidery floss, string, or yarn in various complimentary colors**
- **White glue**
- **Binder clips**

String Art Board

Create geometrical masterpieces with a String Art Boards. String Art was considered very groovy back in the 1970s, and it is a good way to learn about lines and curves in interesting patterns. Plus, you can use String Art to add pizazz to drab walls.

Mother & Daughter: *String up a word that best describes you and your mom. Add colors, shapes, and patterns that best describe your word.*

Make It!

MAKE THE CANVAS

1. Glue the four layers of cardboard together. Use binder clips to hold the layers together as it dries. This will serve as the canvas for your string art.

2. Paint your cardboard a base color, like pink or white.

3. Glue the ribbon around the edge to create a border/frame.

START PINNING

1. Choose a word, phrase, letter, or shape and draw it on your template paper. See some suggestions at right.

2. Cut out the letters and/or shapes and tape them to the cardboard.

3. Push the map pins into your cardboard along the edge of your paper template.

   • They should be evenly spaced (about ½" [1.3 cm] apart).

   • Be sure not to push the pins down all the way; allow enough space so you can wrap your string under the pin heads.

4. Continue pushing pins into the cardboard until you have completely outlined all your letters and shapes.

5. Remove the paper templates.

6. Place map pins around the edge of all four sides of your cardboard, making a border.

7. You can also place pins randomly between your letters/shapes and the border.

String Time

1. Wrap one end of the embroidery floss around a corner map pin twice and then tightly tie a double knot. Trim the thread as close to the knot as possible.

2. Outline the letters and shapes first by wrapping the string around each pin before you move on to the next. Keep your floss taut between each pin so it stays in place.

3. Make a crisscross pattern (random or organized) until the string covers the desired areas.

4. When you're done, tie off the string to a pin and trim the thread as close to the knot as possible.

Some words and shapes to consider making:

Make it personal
• Your name
• Your initials
• Your age
• The shape of your home state

Words and phrases
• Love
• Peace
• O.K.
• I ♥ U
• Create
• Believe
• Dream big
• Joy
• LOL
• 4ever
• Hi5
• BFF

Shapes and icons
• Hearts
• Stars
• Arrows
• Triangles
• Circles
• Chevron

Tip
Put a coat of your favorite color nail polish on the head of each pin so they match!

You'll Need

- Empty thread spool
- **Decorative paper** (use some of the paper on pages 141, 143, or your own)
- **Embroidery floss, string, yarn, or ribbon**
- **2 buttons** (one slightly smaller than the other)
- **3 to 4 decorative beads**
- Scissors or craft knife
- Ruler
- White glue
- Pen, markers, or pencils
- Tapestry needle
- Hot-glue gun and glue sticks

Spool Gift-Tag Ornament

Make a homemade gift that is truly spooled from the heart! Spool Gift Tags are a great way to tell that special someone how much you care in an unwinding and creative way.

Mother & Daughter: *Turn your spool into a memory scroll. Write down and record all of your milestones. Make your paper strip extra long so you have room to include all of your best memories. Don't forget to write down the date. What a great way to end the year!*

Make It!

1. Cut a strip of decorative paper that is the slightly smaller than the height of your spool. You should be able to wrap it snugly without bending the edges.

2. Write your message on the strip.

3. Take the left end of your paper strip and thread a piece of embroidery floss or ribbon through it. You will use this thread to "close" your note and attach it to the spool. Tie a knot where it meets the paper, string a bead, and tie another knot to secure it.

4. Glue the right end of your paper strip to the spool and allow the glue to dry.

5. Tightly wrap the strip of paper around the spool.

6. Wind the floss a few times and tie it into a bow and around the bead.

7. Double-thread your tapestry needle with a piece of string and tie a knot at the end.

8. Thread the string first through your decorative beads, then the bottom of the spool, and finally up through the buttons.

9. Tie a knot close to the top button and you are done. Hot glue your buttons in place if they are wobbly.

Tips

If you have an extra-long message, splice two strips of paper together with tape to make the strip long enough to hold the entire thought.

Consider the message possibilities:

- The gift recipient's name
- Happy Birthday
- Happy [insert holiday here]
- A favorite quote, poem, or music lyric
- Your wish for the New Year
- A secret message
- A good thought for a new year
- Love, peace, happiness
- Mazol tov!
- It's your day!
- Thank you
- Joy
- Love

You'll Need

- **A jar** (mason, baby food, peanut butter, jam, or pasta sauce jars all work well)
- **Fine to chunky glitter** (the finer glitter will be suspended longer and takes longer to fall)
- **Distilled water**
- **Glycerin** (available at your local pharmacy)
- **Sequins** (optional)
- **Food coloring** (optional)
- **Patterned paper** (use some of the paper on pages 141, 143, or your own)
- **Paint**
- **Decoupage or homemade wheat paste**
- **Hot-glue gun and glue sticks**
- **Scissors or craft knife**
- **Decorative accessories:** String, ribbon, and trim

Peaceful Mind Globe

What a great way to relieve stress when you are feeling upset and overwhelmed. A Peaceful Mind Globe is easy to make and just the perfect thing to provide calm after a tough day.

Mother & Daughter: *Shake some peace into a tough conversation. Use your peaceful mind globe as a time out and wait for all the flakes to fall before you resume your discussion.*

Make It!

1. Clean your jar fully. Scrape off the label and glue.
2. Fill the jar up to the rim with distilled water.
3. Add a drop or two of food coloring (See calming color choices at right).
4. Mix in 2 to 5 drops of glycerin. The glycerin will suspend the glitter flakes so they will fall more slowly. A little goes a long way.
5. Add in glitter and optional sequins.
6. Apply a bead of hot glue onto the rim of your jar and screw on the lid.
7. Add another bead of glue around the edge of the lid to seal it shut.
8. Decorate and paint the lid of the jar as you like.

Use it! When you are feeling anxious, afraid, or stressed before a big test, turn the jar over and shake. Gaze at the jar and watch the flakes fall while you clear your mind. You will start to relax. Visualize your swirling thoughts slowing down and settling to the bottom.

Choose Calming Colors

CALMING COLORS:

GREENS: *(elements: earth & water)* restful, fresh, rejuvenating, tranquil, calm

BLUES: *(elements: air & water)* sky, water, serenity, cool, healing

PINKS: *(element: fire)* soft, tranquil, peaceful, balance

PURPLES: *(element: water)* strength, wisdom, inner peace

SILVER: *(element: air)* sophisticated, elegant, neutral

GOLDS AND YELLOWS: *(element: earth)* cheerful, optimistic, helps concentration

WHITE: *(element: air)* clarity, reflective, purity, open

RESOURCES

East Bay Depot for Creative Reuse
www.creativereuse.org

I can't even begin to tell you how many supplies for this book came from here. From baby jars to Altoid tins to an endless supply of fabric, ribbon, buttons, beads, and yarn. This place is an ecological treasure trove of art and craft supplies. Their mission is to "increase the awareness of school children and the general public regarding the green benefits of reusing materials" by diverting waste from landfills and collecting and redistributing discarded goods as low-cost supplies for art, education, and social services. Check the Directory of Creative Reuse Centers to see if there is one located in your community. www.lancastercreativereuse.org/directory-creative-reuse-centers.html

Freecycle
www.freecycle.org

This is a global grassroots movement that helps you find local folks who are giving and getting stuff for free in their communities. It's a great place to get free arts and craft supplies from people who no longer want or need them. Freecycle's mission is "to build a worldwide gifting movement that reduces waste, saves precious resources, and eases the burden on our landfills while enabling our members to benefit from the strength of a larger community."

Urban Ore

http://urbanore.com

I found the silver spoons I used for garden markers here. This is one of my favorite Bay Area resources for those hard-to-find things that you might not even know you want or need. And how cool is it that on an average day Urban Ore prevents nearly 20 tons of waste from entering our landfills?

The Alameda Point Antiques Faire (or as I call it, The Alameda Flea Market)

http://alamedapointantiquesfaire.com

This is one of Ava Blu's and my favorite things to do together on the first Sunday of the month. Just walking this flea market is an amazing source of inspiration. I can't tell you how many treasures we have carried home from here, one of our favorite's being a crystal ball that hangs from our window and creates rainbows from the afternoon light.

Check the US Flea Market Directory to find a market in your state and locate city.
http://collectors.org/FM/

Staples

www.staples.com

Map pins, stickers, and labels. I love reinventing office supplies into fun art projects.

Michael's

www.michaels.com

It's my go-to craft store for everything else I may need, from paint, foam brushes, embroidery floss, glue, beads, jewelry blanks, and hot-glue sticks. I always walk out of there with a full bag of supplies and usually more than I need.

Craigslist.org

www.craigslist.org

My goodness–what can't you find here for low or no cost? Not only have I found, collected, and given away free supplies on Craigslist, but I've also bought furniture, found jobs, and rented houses through Craigslist. It's an amazing resource to find just about anything you might need.

And don't forget to rummage through your home, local garage sales, flea markets, auctions, and thrift shops. These are great places to find green and inexpensive treasures and supplies that you can upcycle!

Avia Venefica's Whats-Your-Sign

www.whats-your-sign.com

Interpreting the meaning behind symbols, signs, elements, animals, and colors is definitely a very personal and subjective decision. Avia's website is my go-to resource for all things symbolic! All the information she provides is well-researched. You can easily tell she is passionate about what she shares. It's a great starting point to learn about the symbolic meaning behind almost anything you may be wondering about.

ACKNOWLEDGMENTS

I cannot put into words how much help and support Myleen Obando has provided or what it has meant to me. This book never would have come about if it weren't for her guidance and cheerleading. From the early stages of helping me brainstorm the book proposal, to her continuous input on the craft ideas, not to mention spending time with me to go through each activity step by step to make sure the directions were clear while watching me make some of these crafts via Skype. Myleen helped lift me up and push me forward. I feel so lucky to have her not only as a cousin, but also as a co-creative conspirator.

To my editor, Mary Ann Hall, for reaching out and being patient enough to go through two book proposals with me and giving me the opportunity to write, create, and make this book a reality. We have travelled this journey together.

To my wonderful photographer and friend, Stefanie Reneé. Your pictures brought this book to life! Your dazzling visual displays show the joy of Just Us Girls crafting, playing, and connecting.

To Ava Blu, my daughter: without you this never would have been dreamed of. You are an inspiration with your beautiful dreams and amazing imagination. You are always up for making a spectacular mess with me! Art can be messy, but that's what sometimes makes it fun. Thank you for being patient with Mama, taking your time to listen and follow the directions. Crafting side-by-side with you is one of my favorite things to do. I love listening to your wonderful ideas and especially when you model your crafty creations! I like to think that when you are grown, you will look back at this book with fond memories of us creating and crafting beautiful things together.

To my parents for always encouraging and supporting my art. Even when it was unconventional and I painted my childhood bedroom. (I'm still not sorry about that.)

To Jay, my partner and husband. Thank you for handling all of the grown-up stuff and being my rock when I was floating in my creative sea. You endure my "burning the late night oil" crafting crazes and Ava Blu and I displaying all of our "girlie" crafts throughout the house. You are our number one craft curator, supporter, and my best friend.

And a huge THANK YOU to all of the girls, moms, and daughters who crafted, modeled, assisted, and helped out with all of our natural and upcycled treasures.

Ava Blu · Kate · Myleen & Cindy

Parker, Jeanne & Margot

Laura & Jett

Penelope, Stefanie & Kadison

Ella, Kristin & Paige

Mary Ann & Alexandra

Susan, Sasha & Bonnie

Shalom & Annika

Jennifer, Cadence & Sophia

Kadison, Ava Blu, Ariella & Cindy Ann

Jueli, Ariella & Marlene

Sam & Melissa

Josie, Aurora, DeVonne & Bailey

ABOUT THE AUTHOR

Cindy Ann is an artist and illustrator who is known for coloring outside of the lines and on the walls! Originally from the east coast, she now calls the Bay Area home. Her past experiences have enriched her love for creating beautiful things. For over thirteen years Cindy Ann worked as an art director and design manager in the corporate world by day while pursuing her creative endeavors by night. Her corporate influences include Old Navy, Chronicle Books, Klutz, Time, Inc., and Papyrus. In Spring of 2011, Cindy Ann said, "Adieu!" to corporate life and opened the studio doors full-time to Blu Penny by Cindy Ann :: Artist, Blogger, and Mama.

Outside of the studio, you can find Cindy Ann exploring her local hiking trails, crafting and baking brownies with her daughter, Ava Blu, husband, Jay, and Boston Terrier, Penny. Come and Live the Life Creative with Cindy Ann! Visit www.BluPenny.com to learn how.

PHOTO BY THEA COUGHLIN

Stefanie Reneé is a lifestyle photographer based in the Bay Area. She is all about natural light and finding that glimmer of magic in everyone. www.stefanierenee.net

Myleen Obando is a communicator and brand strategist based in South Florida. She connects the dots and declutters the visual chaos for business owners to have those AHA! moments. www.ClearCreativeCommunication.com

TEAR-OUT INSTRUCTIONS: Tear out desired pages, and then use scissors to cut apart smaller designs as needed.

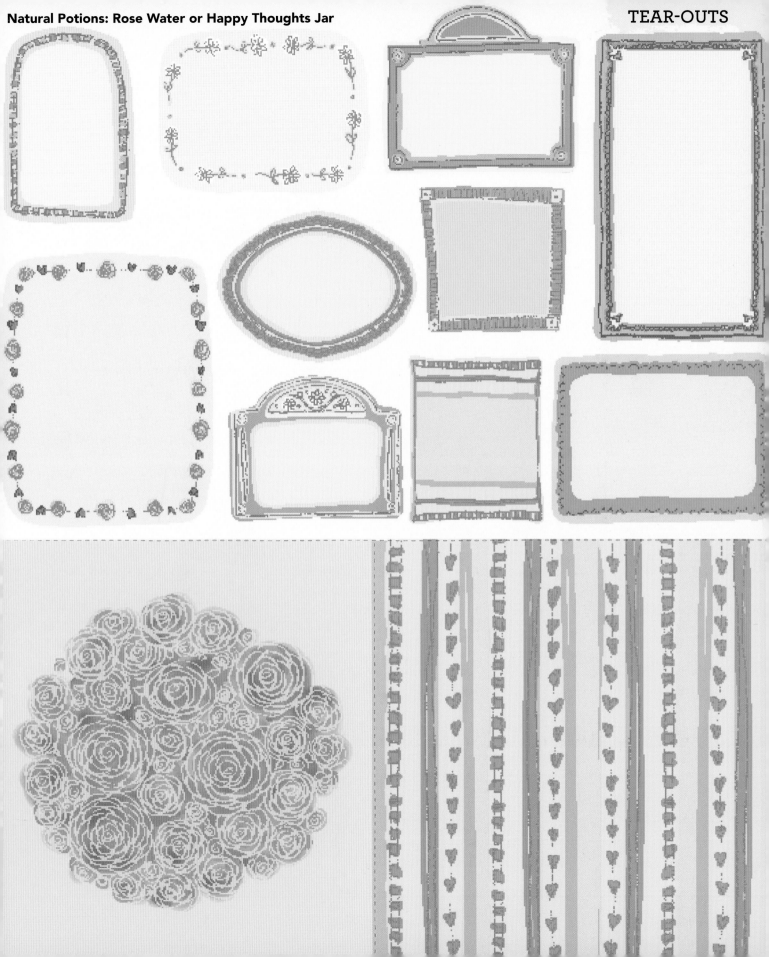

Tablespoon

Teaspoon

Spoon Garden Markers

Spoon Garden Markers

The Huntress: Bow & Arrows

Badge & Ribbon Medallions

Badge & Ribbon Medallions

Rock Games

Punched Tin-Can Lanterns

1.

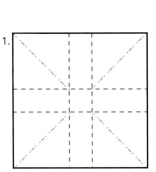

4 Mountain and 4 Valley Folds

Mountain Fold

- - - - -

Valley Fold

- · - · -

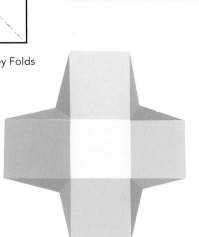

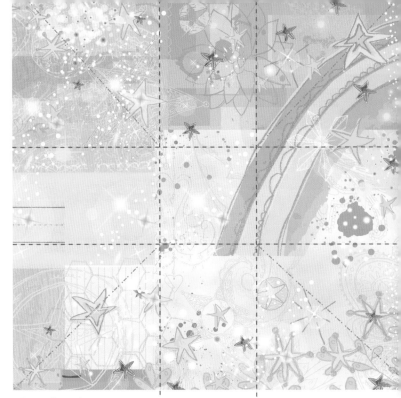

Front/Inside

2.

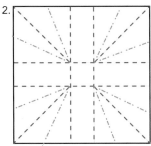

2 Valley Folds and 1 Mountain Fold in each corner

Fold in to form corners

3.

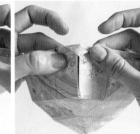

Fold each triangle over the corners.

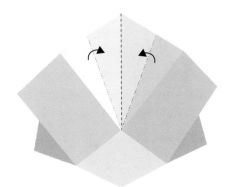

Lightbulb Hot-Air Balloon Ornament

Lightbulb Hot-Air Balloon Ornament
Back/Inside

Woodland Animal Masks

Left Bunny Ear

Right Bunny Ear

Summer Fairies (Front)

Summer Fairies (Back)